THE BEDFORD SERIES IN HISTORY AND CULTURE

Politics and Society in Japan's Meiji Restoration

A Brief History with Documents

THE BEDFORD SERIES IN HISTORY AND CULTURE

Politics and Society in Japan's Meiji Restoration

A Brief History with Documents

Anne Walthall

University of California, Irvine

M. William Steele

International Christian University

bedford/st.martin's
Macmillan Learning

Boston | New York

For Bedford/St. Martin's

Vice President, Editorial, Macmillan Learning Humanities: Edwin Hill
Publisher for History: Michael Rosenberg
Acquiring Editor for History: Laura Arcari
Director of Development for History: Jane Knetzger
Assistant Editor: Melanie McFadyen
History Marketing Manager: Melissa Famiglietti
Production Editor: Lidia MacDonald-Carr
Production Supervisor: Robert Cherry
Director of Rights and Permissions: Hilary Newman
Permissions Associate: Michael McCarty
Permissions Manager: Kalina Ingham
Cover Design: William Boardman
Cover Photo: (Front cover) *Children Playing King of the Mountain and Setting Off Firecrackers,* 1868. Courtesy Hachiro Yuasa Memorial Museum; (Anne Walthall photo) Courtesy Robert G. Moeller; (M. William Steele photo) Patricia Sippel
Project Management: Books By Design, Inc.
Cartographer: Mapping Specialists, Ltd.
Composition: Achorn International, Inc.
Printing and Binding: LSC Communications

Manufactured in the United States of America.

1   0   9   8   7   6
f   e   d   c   b   a

For information, write: Bedford/St. Martin's, 75 Arlington Street, Boston, MA 02116
(617-399-4000)

ISBN 978-1-4576-8105-9

About the Cover: "Children Playing King of the Mountain and Setting Off Firecrackers," 1868. Depictions of King of the Mountain, a popular children's game, were used to portray the war between the imperial forces (led by Satsuma and Chōshū domains) and defenders of the Tokugawa regime. This print was probably issued soon after the Battle of Ueno Hill on July 4, 1868, that resulted in undisputed imperial control of the city, soon to be renamed Tokyo—the Eastern Capital. On top of the mountain, boys representing Satsuma and Chōshū (who holds a baby—the emperor—aloft) proclaim victory. The battle was decided by superior firepower, especially the Armstrong cannon. The exploding firecrackers recall the roar of the cannon, the barrage of rifle shots, and the ensuing fire that engulfed the northeastern section of Edo on that fateful summer day.

Acknowledgments

Text acknowledgments and copyrights appear at the back of the book on page 162. Art acknowledgments and copyrights appear on the same page as art selections they cover; these acknowledgments and copyrights constitute an extension of the copyright page.

At the time of publication all Internet URLs published in this text were found to accurately link to their intended Web site. If you do find a broken link, please forward the information to history@macmillan.com so that it can be corrected for the next printing.

Foreword

The Bedford Series in History and Culture is designed so that readers can study the past as historians do.

The historian's first task is finding the evidence. Documents, letters, memoirs, interviews, pictures, movies, novels, or poems can provide facts and clues. Then the historian questions and compares the sources. There is more to do than in a courtroom, for hearsay evidence is welcome, and the historian is usually looking for answers beyond act and motive. Different views of an event may be as important as a single verdict. How a story is told may yield as much information as what it says.

Along the way the historian seeks help from other historians and perhaps from specialists in other disciplines. Finally, it is time to write, to decide on an interpretation and how to arrange the evidence for readers.

Each book in this series contains an important historical document or group of documents, each document a witness from the past and open to interpretation in different ways. The documents are combined with some element of historical narrative—an introduction or a biographical essay, for example—that provides students with an analysis of the primary source material and important background information about the world in which it was produced.

Each book in the series focuses on a specific topic within a specific historical period. Each provides a basis for lively thought and discussion about several aspects of the topic and the historian's role. Each is short enough (and inexpensive enough) to be a reasonable one-week assignment in a college course. Whether as classroom or personal reading, each book in the series provides firsthand experience of the challenge—and fun—of discovering, recreating, and interpreting the past.

Lynn Hunt
David W. Blight
Bonnie G. Smith

Preface

In the nineteenth-century age of reform, revolution, and imperialism, Japan was the first non-Western country to transform its government while fending off foreign domination. How did this happen? Was it simply a matter of geopolitics, or was there something about Japan that made it more amenable to change and better able to resist outside pressure? What were the consequences of engaging in new forms of diplomacy for Japan's state and society and for Japan's relations with the rest of the world? To address these questions, we examine the events leading up to the Meiji Restoration of 1868, when a 250-year-old military regime was replaced by a government headed by the Meiji emperor.

The response of each nation to nineteenth-century state formation depended on a host of domestic factors: the composition of the ruling class and the relationship between ruler and ruled, plus the degree and type of economic development, social integration, and cultural expression. We also know that history matters. When Japan's ruling classes jettisoned the previous regime, which granted considerable autonomy to local rulers, they reached back into the country's ancient past to find a model of direct rule by the emperor. Above all was the question of national identity: How did people see themselves, their relations with one another, and their position vis-à-vis the rest of the world? By focusing on Japan, this volume offers both a case study for considering these issues and an opportunity to examine the factors that made it possible for Japan to retain its sovereignty.

Part One provides the historical context for students to grasp the significance of the documents in Part Two. It describes a complex political landscape with multiple overlapping centers of authority: a society shackled by a system of hereditary occupations and status, a thriving commercial economy that did not prevent famines, and a flourishing cultural milieu that allowed space for commentary on current events. This introduction traces the history of the period, starting in 1825, when an influential intellectual, Aizawa Seishisai, wrote a treatise warning that foreigners threatened Japan's moral fabric. The years that followed were filled with unrest and attempts at political reform. When Commodore Matthew Perry arrived with a letter from U.S. president Millard Fillmore offering friendship and amity in 1853, it sparked debate and criticism among people outside government circles. As the political crisis deepened, it engulfed ever larger segments of the population. Amid attempts at forging new political alignments, some men became radicalized, while others proposed military, political, economic, and social reforms. Like all attempts at national integration, the Meiji Restoration brought bloodshed in its train. Even after the last battle had been fought and a course toward centralization and engagement in world affairs charted, the consequences for ordinary people were mixed.

The documents in Part Two trace the evolving political situation, illustrate changes in society, and give voice to ordinary people. A number of them have not appeared previously in English or are scattered in obscure publications. We selected these documents with two goals in mind. The first was to introduce students to how Japanese people in the nineteenth century thought and acted in dealing with foreign pressure and domestic discord. The second was to encourage students to think about the global phenomenon of national consolidation by analyzing one example of how it came about. The documents are arranged chronologically to guide students through the events that marked this period of tumultuous change, and the headnote to each document will help students place it in context. By juxtaposing different types of texts and visual documents, we hope to give students a feel for how events in various contexts each had its own significance.

This volume also includes several maps to help students locate places mentioned in the documents. At the end of the book, the chronology places the documents in a broader historical context. Questions for consideration invite students to consider linkages among the texts and between issues specific to Japan and the broader topics of nineteenth-century imperialism and national consolidation. Finally, the bibliography lists important works in English on the years leading up to the Meiji Restoration.

A NOTE ON THE TEXT

All Japanese names are given in the Japanese word order: surname first followed by personal name. All dates have been converted to the Gregorian (Western) calendar. Macrons are used to indicate long vowels.

ACKNOWLEDGMENTS

Series advisory editor Bonnie Smith first proposed this topic to us and then shepherded it along its path to publication. Without her encouragement and help, this book would not exist. We would also like to thank Patricia Sippel and Kate Wildman Nakai for keeping us on track and Andrew Steele for his help in researching the maps.

The following reviewers made many valuable suggestions: Theodore F. Cook, William Paterson University; Denis Gainty, Georgia State University; Sue Gronewold, Kean University; Chau J. Kelly, University of North Florida; Laura Nenzi, University of Tennessee; Kenneth Orosz, Buffalo State College; Michael Rutz, University of Wisconsin Oshkosh; Kenneth Swope, University of Southern Mississippi; Shane Tomashot, Georgia State University; and Michael Wert, Marquette University.

At Bedford/St. Martin's, the following people contributed to bringing this volume to fruition: Publisher for History Michael Rosenberg; Acquiring Editor for History Laura Arcari; Director of Development for History Jane Knetzger; History Marketing Manager Melissa Famiglietti; Assistant Editor and Developmental Editor Melanie McFadyen; Production Editor Lidia MacDonald-Carr; Cover Designer William Boardman; and Production Coordinator Nancy Benjamin of Books By Design.

Anne Walthall and M. William Steele

Contents

Maps, Table, and Illustrations

Map 1. *Japan in the Early Nineteenth Century*

PART ONE

Introduction: Domestic Disorder, Imperialism, and National Consolidation

In 1868 Japan's emperor announced to the world that the shogunate, the military regime that had governed Japan in his stead for 265 years, had been abolished. Henceforth, the emperor himself would exercise supreme authority in all the nation's internal and external affairs. By 1871 some 280 semiautonomous states, or domains, led by hereditary lords known as daimyo had been replaced by 72 prefectures run by governors appointed by the emperor. This change, known as the Meiji Restoration, marked the culmination of decades-long domestic turmoil and launched a process of national integration and unification. Since it was equally the result of attempts to fend off Western domination, it can be seen as beginning Japan's active participation in international affairs. How did the restoration happen? How did political power come to coalesce around the emperor? And what did national consolidation mean for Japanese society?

By the early nineteenth century, macroeconomic changes that foreshadowed Japan's formidable presence in world affairs at the end of the century were under way. First, Japan had benefitted from over two hundred years of peace and economic growth. The population had more than doubled (from around 12 million in 1600 to over 25 million in the 1820s), agricultural productivity had risen even more dramatically, and the quality of life of ordinary Japanese people had improved greatly.[1] Second, people were moving into urban centers. Already by the turn of the eighteenth century, Edo was the largest city in the world, bustling with a

1

dynamic cultural life. Third, the spread of literacy and a commercial revolution brought what is sometimes termed proto-industrialization to rural areas. Transportation networks on land and sea carried people and goods across the country.[2] Finally, although loyalty to village or domain and suspicion of strangers from different regions remained strong, there was a growing national consciousness. Economic, religious, scholarly, and cultural communication networks that crossed domain boundaries mitigated political fragmentation. One message carried by these networks, for example, was that the military ruled in the emperor's name; everyone, including the military, had the duty to serve the emperor.

While the political elite saw some of these changes as opportunities, they regarded most as challenges to existing institutions and ways of thinking that threatened their authority and their ability to maintain national security and stability. This is where our story begins.

SACRED RULERS AND MILITARY REGIMES

Early-nineteenth-century scholars who studied Japan's origins traced the emperor's lineage in an unbroken line back to the sun goddess, Amaterasu, who sent her imperial grandson Jimmu down from the high plain of heaven to govern Japan. In their vision of the ancient state, the emperor's decrees matched the intentions of the gods, and his administration united worship and rule. Bridging the gap between the seen world of humankind and the unseen world of the gods, the emperor was himself a manifest god. Lest his august mind be sullied by the impure world of human affairs, his aristocratic advisers took over the actual management of the kingdom. Beginning in the late twelfth century, three successive military regimes left the rituals of rule to the emperor and his court, while they took over the substance.

The third military regime began in 1603 when Tokugawa Ieyasu had the imperial court invest him with the title *sei-i tai shōgun* (barbarian-subduing generalissimo).[3] Building on self-governing communities created during the preceding century of civil war and determined to maintain military preparedness, the new regime enforced policies designed to slot people, high and low, into a hereditary status system (Table 1). Although each status had a specific social function, individuals within it might pursue diverse livelihoods. The shogun confined the emperor and his court to the ancient capital of Kyoto and ordered them to devote their time to the study of Japan's classics. The Tokugawa directly administered lands scat-

Table 1. *The Social and Political Structure in Early-Nineteenth-Century Japan*

THE RULING CLASS		
IN KYOTO	IN EDO	IN DOMAINS
Emperor Court nobility	Shogun Samurai (warriors)	Daimyo (lords) Samurai (warriors)

COMMONERS	
URBAN	RURAL
Merchants, artisans, actors, doctors, maids, sales girls, prostitutes, priests, day laborers, beggars, outcasts	Farmers, tenant farmers, fishers, priests, hunters, miners, outcasts

tered throughout Japan that produced approximately 15 percent of the country's total agricultural tax base. It also controlled the major cities of Osaka (the country's marketing center) and Nagasaki (open to foreign trade), the mines that produced the metal for Japan's coinage, the sea transport and national road system that linked all parts of Japan to its capital at Edo, and foreign affairs. The domains of the daimyo (some 280 of them) remained self-governing, with their own laws, currencies, armed forces, and treasuries. All daimyo were required to perform a biannual tour of duty in Edo, where they had to swear fealty to the shogun and sit in his audience chambers approximately three times a month. The rest of the time, they were to administer their domains. Their mothers, wives, and heirs resided full time in Edo as hostages to ensure the daimyo's loyalty. The costs of travel and maintaining plural households led to grave financial problems that left many domains on the verge of bankruptcy. Although this allowed the shogunate to increase its power over the daimyo, local and regional identities remained strong well into Japan's modern era.

The Tokugawa shoguns divided the daimyo into three groups. They entrusted those who had fought for Ieyasu during his rise to national hegemony, the vassal daimyo, with running the shogun's vast administrative apparatus and making policy. They were the ones who dealt with domestic problems and foreign pressure. Another group consisted of daimyo given privileged access to the shogun because they were related to him. Tokugawa Nariaki, the lord of Mito, used his special position as the descendant of Ieyasu's eleventh son to offer unwanted advice on foreign affairs. Many in the last group, the outside daimyo, whose support for Ieyasu had been less than enthusiastic, had large domains as far from Edo as possible. They were not supposed to have any voice in policy, even though some played important roles in foreign affairs. In 1868 their troops fought under the imperial banner against the shogun's supporters.

During the century of civil war before the Tokugawa period, each daimyo amassed the largest army he could afford. Because military service was a lifetime commitment, soldiers—the men we now call samurai—continued in the positions held by their ancestors when peace came. Like daimyo and shoguns, samurai were members of the ruling class. After two centuries of peace, however, many of their military functions were redundant and sometimes a financial burden. Over time they became increasingly literate and functioned as skilled administrators; knowledge of the literary arts was deemed equal in importance to martial skills. They also developed a code of conduct that stressed the virtues of loyalty to superiors, compassion to those below, and good manners. Some historians have pointed out that by 1868 they constituted a valuable reservoir of bureaucratic expertise. Others emphasize that the warriors' desire to have their talents recognized through promotion to higher offices than was permitted by their hereditary status constituted a powerful impetus for change.

The hereditary status system divided commoners—the members of the ruled class—based on residence and male occupation. Women were not presumed to have an occupation of their own, and they were discouraged from acting independently of their families. Not all women could or would follow these dictates. Farmers, who constituted around 85 percent of the population, lived in agrarian villages. They had a great deal of autonomy in running their own affairs, but they were expected to stay put. Rulers levied taxes on villages, not individuals, and when farmers thought the taxes were too heavy, they organized mass demonstrations to complain. By the early nineteenth century, they had many opportunities to earn income besides growing food. They might grow tea or cotton, raise silkworms, make paper, or harvest lacquer sap to coat wood products. Some farmers grew rich by acting as middlemen or distributors; others ended up so poor that they were reduced to tenancy or sharecropping—and sometimes to starvation. When Japan allowed foreign trade in the late 1850s, agrarian products such as the silk and tea produced largely by farm women were major export items.

Approximately 15 percent of the population lived in early-nineteenth-century cities and castle towns (the headquarters of the daimyo domains), making Japan one of the most urbanized countries in the premodern world.[4] In addition to samurai, urban spaces contained artisans and merchants, who provided necessities and luxury items to the ruling class—and increasingly to each other, as well as entertainers, male and female. As in the countryside, extremes of wealth and poverty existed cheek by jowl. Although not all merchants belonged to the same economic class, they all belonged to the same social status. Moving from one status to another was officially forbidden, though known to happen. The townspeople enjoyed a sophisticated culture of books, music, theater, and woodblock prints. They bought and sold information about the ruling class and enjoyed satirical verses that commented on contemporary events. Townspeople and rural folk had no formal say over public policy, but as we will see, they had ways to convince government to take their interests into account.

Tokugawa Ieyasu and his successors tried to craft a political order that would endure because it stifled conflict, but their hopes proved ill founded. By the early eighteenth century, the economic solvency of the ruling class was under siege. Hereditary samurai stipends lost value as agrarian productivity increased along with the cost of goods and services. In this way, the development of a commercial economy benefitted farmers and merchants relatively more than samurai, who lived on fixed incomes. In addition, the threat of protests and other factors restricted tax increases. Merchants who were expected to bow down before their military betters flaunted their wealth. In the 1720s and 1730s, the eighth shogun, Yoshimune, launched a series of reforms to shore up samurai's income by manipulating the price of rice (stipends were paid in rice, which then had to be converted to coinage), issuing sumptuary legislation that tied the quality of clothing to status, and otherwise urging everyone to be frugal. These measures were called the Kyōhō reforms because they took place during the Kyōhō era (1716–1735). At the end of the eighteenth century, the shogunate launched a second series of reforms, the Kansei reforms (1789–1800), which ordered frugality, canceled ruling-class debts, and tried to send migrants in Edo back to their home villages. Daimyo also took steps to strengthen their finances, from promoting specialty products in order to increase revenues to cutting samurai stipends in an attempt to reduce costs. The status system established at the beginning of the dynasty proved porous as time went on. To many members of the ruling class, it appeared that wealth tended to flow to the bottom of society rather than rising to the top.

FOREIGN AFFAIRS

Tokugawa policies regulating foreign affairs also proved increasingly difficult to enforce in the early nineteenth century. The sixteenth century had brought Western traders into the mix of Southeast Asian, Chinese, and Korean ships that visited Japan's harbors, and Japanese seamen had set up residences as far afield as Vietnam and Thailand. Among them were merchant adventurers, called *wakō* (Japanese pirates) by Chinese and Koreans. In an effort to combat piracy, enhance official control over foreign trade, and restrict outside contacts, the shogunate summoned home all Japanese expatriates in 1635 with a warning that if they lingered abroad, they would never be allowed to return. In addition, it forbade the building of oceangoing ships. Small vessels could haul cargo and go after fish, but they hardly sufficed for deep-sea voyages, as many a shipwrecked sailor learned to his cost.

Then there were the Catholic missionaries, blamed for having so weakened the Filipino population with their foreign creed that the Philippines became easy prey for Spanish conquest. As the Protestant Dutch were only too happy to point out, Catholic Christianity required loyalty not to local gods or rulers but to a universal god and the pope. The Tokugawa shogunate issued increasingly stringent laws against missionary work, forbade the practice of the Christian faith, and massacred converts. In 1639 it banned all Westerners but the Dutch from trade with Japan and confined the Dutch to Dejima, a tiny man-made island in Nagasaki Bay.

The shogunate also regulated trade with its neighbors. In the north, it set up an office to handle relations with the Ainu and anyone else who ventured into Hokkaido. The Sō daimyo who ruled the Tsushima Islands had greater prominence than their tiny domain warranted because they served as middlemen between Korea and Japan. In 1609 Satsuma, a domain at the southern tip of Kyushu, invaded the kingdom of the Ryūkyū Islands (with its headquarters on the island of Okinawa). In return for leaving the Ryukyuan king in place, Satsuma assumed suzerainty over Ryukyuan affairs, while tacitly recognizing Ryukyuan tribute missions to China. Chinese merchants also received permission to trade in Nagasaki, where their numbers exceeded those of the Dutch.

In the late eighteenth century, the Russians posed a new challenge to this system. Having explored Siberia and claimed it for the Russian tsar, adventurers, fishermen, and traders traversed the Kamchatka Peninsula, Sakhalin Island, and the Kurile Islands before approaching Hokkaido. In 1792 an envoy from the Russian court, Adam Laxman, arrived in Hokkaido with two Japanese castaways who had spent ten years in Russia.

Laxman wanted to travel to Edo and open trade relations with the shogun's government, but he was courteously refused. Instead, he received a document saying that Russia might send one ship to Nagasaki to discuss trade issues. His visit startled Japanese officials and intellectuals. The shogun and his ministers interviewed the former castaways, and reports of their experience circulated widely. Men inside and outside the government offered proposals for how to meet the Russian threat.

Although Russia made an unsuccessful attempt to follow up on Laxman's visit in 1804, it soon left the field to the British and Americans. Four years later, the British frigate HMS *Phaeton* sailed into Nagasaki Bay in search of Dutch ships. (The Netherlands was then under the control of Napoleon Bonaparte, with whom Britain was at war.) The regular trading season having ended, the *Phaeton* caught the Japanese defenders off guard. The shogun's magistrate hastily summoned troops from the domains assigned to protect the port, but they arrived after the *Phaeton*'s commander had landed troops, surveyed the defenses, demanded supplies at gunpoint, and sailed off. This brazen exploit so humiliated the magistrate that he committed suicide.

During the early nineteenth century, American and British ships crisscrossed the Pacific in search of whales. The area around Hokkaido, in the North Pacific, was a particularly bountiful whaling ground. To render whale blubber into oil, the whalers needed firewood. To keep their crews free from scurvy (a vitamin C deficiency), they needed fresh water and food. Japan was ideally situated to supply these goods. Whalers came so frequently into the seas off Japan that Japanese fishermen sometimes traded with them without bothering to inform officials. In 1823 British sailors landed on an island off the coast of Kyushu, demanded rice, and stole a cow. In 1824 a different group landed on the Mito coast northeast of Edo, in search of provisions. They were captured, held for two weeks, and interrogated before being returned to their ships with orders never to return.[5]

Neither the British nor the Russians had permission to trade in Nagasaki, let alone the rest of Japan, and their disregard for existing regulations made the shogunate increasingly uneasy. In 1825 the shogunate decided to turn threat into policy by issuing an unprecedented order to close the country: "Whenever a foreign ship is sighted approaching any point on our coast, all persons on hand should fire on it and drive it off."[6] Unlike earlier edicts that merely urged local rulers to persuade foreigners to depart, this one explicitly encouraged the use of force. The decree provided the justification for rejecting later requests for trade by British and American ships, but it ultimately proved unenforceable. News that British forces had defeated China in the Opium War of 1839–1842 so shocked Japan's rulers that the shogunate agreed to relax the expulsion edict to the extent of allowing foreign ships to acquire firewood and water. Nonetheless, many feared that victory over once mighty China, the fount of civilization, meant that foreign imperialists would soon turn on Japan.

DOMESTIC TURMOIL

Like many members of the ruling class, Aizawa Seishisai had a low opinion of commoners. When he wrote his *Shinron* (*New Theses*) in 1825 (Document 1), he saw the threat from the West as being both ideological and military because, he feared, it would be easy for foreign barbarians to convert gullible, ignorant people to Christianity. In 1824 he had been sent to the fishing village in Mito, where British sailors had landed in search of provisions. Relying on local informants to help with communication, he learned that the fishermen had more intimate knowledge of foreign ways than he did. Worse, they did not see the foreigners as a visceral threat to Japan's integrity. The only way to counter the foreign propaganda of Christianity, Aizawa believed, was to urge all Japanese to revere the emperor and the gods, and most particularly to preserve the *kokutai*, Japan's national essence, which united lord and subject and distinguished it from all other nations.

Aizawa also blamed the country's rulers for Japan's ills. They had become soft and lazy, and did not succor the people; indeed, they paid no attention to them at all. Although at the time he wrote, Japan was enjoying an era of relative peace and prosperity, its effects were mixed. Townspeople, men and women, had enough disposable income to pay for having their hair fixed, take music lessons, and eat out in restaurants. In the region around Edo and in Mito, where Aizawa was based, however, villages were losing population, as young people fled the hard work of agriculture for easier money in the cities, or joined gangs of gamblers and bandits. Although officials were aware of these social and economic problems, they had little idea of how to solve them, short of issuing widely ignored injunctions to stay put. Other regions had become dependent on monoculture for income, a trend spurred by daimyo to maximize taxes. So long as farmers growing cotton in the Osaka region, for example, could rely on other areas to supply them with food, crop specialization worked. As events in the 1830s were to show, however, Japan's early-nineteenth-century economic boom that had brought prosperity to commoners and some measure of financial relief to rulers was more fragile than it appeared.

Resting as it did on an agrarian foundation, Japan's economy suffered when cold summers brought crop failures for three straight years. Starting in 1833, rice harvests plummeted, and those of other crops were not far behind. Farmers in the northeast were the first to run out of food, but even in more salubrious western regions, famine stalked the land. People ate whatever they could find—leaves, weeds, straw. Merchants who hoarded grain and daimyo who closed the borders of their domains made the crisis worse. Contemporary records report that hundreds of thousands died—a sign of inadequate relief measures.

The years 1833 to 1837 saw acts of protest unprecedented in frequency, scale, and violence. Although merchants were the most frequent targets of attack, sometimes farmers blamed both officials and wealthy commoners for their problems. In Chōshū, tens of thousands of farmers demonstrated against the domain's cotton monopoly before turning their fury on the merchants who benefitted from it. Although they did not kill their enemies, they smashed storehouses and shops, hauled out goods from cloth to rice to saké, and trampled the products in the mud to punish wrongdoing. Similar incidents with participants numbering in the thousands erupted in central and eastern Japan.

Popular protests embarrassed officials, but they were too scattered to challenge the regime, nor was that the participants' goal. They wanted governments to act on their behalf; they wanted redress, not revolution. One incident in 1837, however, constituted a more serious threat.

"To know and not to act is not to know" was the philosophy of Ōshio Heihachirō, a former police inspector and hereditary retainer of the shogun stationed in Osaka. A student of Chinese Confucian teachings, Ōshio believed that samurai should devote themselves to serving their lord, even if it meant working as paper-pushing bureaucrats. In extraordinary situations, however, samurai should attempt to determine what was wrong and take the steps necessary to make things right. Inaction thus became a sign of superficial understanding. When famine struck western Japan and desperate people flooded into Osaka, Ōshio decided that all those who tormented the poor were irredeemably evil and deserved to die. In his call to arms (Document 2), he summoned an army of farmers to attack the city and kill both officials and merchants, burn tax records, and distribute food and clothing to the poor. He did not get far; his army never swelled beyond three hundred men, and although they burned down approximately one-quarter of the city, a scale of destruction not seen for two hundred years, the revolt was quickly suppressed. Ōshio committed suicide.

The trouble in the 1830s led the shogunate to try a new set of reforms designed to deal with the perennial problems of expenditures outpacing revenues, popular unrest, challenges to the shogun's prestige, the decline in public morality, and the fear of foreign invasion. The first decrees in 1841 took aim at commoners' customary pursuits that a good Confucian would find reprehensible (Document 3), in particular those that involved close contact between the sexes. The shogunate also tried to regulate commoners' spending habits and urged everyone to follow the spirit of the Kyōhō and Kansei reforms by being frugal. To demonstrate that it was serious, it arrested women who entertained men in inappropriate settings or dressed extravagantly. It also punished popular novelists, printmakers, and actors for setting a bad example. Later it turned its attention to economic matters, dismissing local administrators who had allowed tax revenues to decline, returning migrants to their home villages, and coercing merchants to make voluntary contributions to the shogun's treasury. It also tried more novel approaches, establishing an office that lent money at low interest to impoverished retainers and trying to lower prices by abolishing the guilds that had monopolized trade between Osaka and Edo.

The next year, the shogunate tried to reassert its authority vis-à-vis the daimyo. It forbade domain monopolies and told moneylenders not to handle coins and currency minted or printed in domains. It proposed a plan to drain a large swamp in order to increase the amount of land under cultivation, with the costs of the project to be borne by the daimyo and the benefits to go to the shogunate. To consolidate its landholdings around Edo and Osaka, it ordered its retainers and the daimyo who held fiefs in those areas to agree to a land swap. In the spring of 1843, the twelfth shogun made a pilgrimage to Nikkō, the site of Ieyasu's tomb, a pilgrimage that no shogun had made for seventy years. Daimyo had to provide the manpower for his escort, they had to guard Edo and the passes leading to it during the excursion, and three of them had to house the shogun in suitable splendor both coming and going. That the procession cost the shogunate and the daimyo an immense amount of time and money demonstrated the reaffirmation of Tokugawa authority.

Historians debate whether these reforms of the Tenpō era (1830–1843) had any lasting impact. Attempts to reform popular morals had no more effect than the prohibition of daimyo monopolies and trade guilds. While the measures taken to reassert the shogun's prestige succeeded in the short run, they angered many daimyo. With the possible exception of Satsuma, reforms initiated at the domain level similarly tended to suffer reversals when they ran afoul of entrenched practice. Yet a number of domains, primarily Mito and those in the southwest, took seriously the need for better defense against foreigners. They stationed samurai in coastal garrisons, trained farmers to fight, bought Western weapons through the Dutch at Nagasaki, and made their own cannons and guns.

During the 1840s, another actor made his appearance when emperor Kōmei challenged the political irrelevancy that had been his ancestors' lot. Aizawa and Ōshio had reminded their audiences that behind the shogun stood the emperor, and Aizawa's lord, Tokugawa Nariaki, called for the shogun to show his respect for the emperor by restoring imperial tombs. In 1841 the emperor proposed that his predecessor be given honors unheard-of since the tenth century because he had revived ancient ceremonies. These honors required shogunal approval, which was politically difficult to withhold. In 1846 the court sent an imperial rescript to Edo ordering the shogunate to strengthen coastal defenses and to keep it informed on foreign affairs. Since the shogunate had told the court about conflicts with the Russians in Hokkaido in 1807, it had inadvertently set a precedent for imperial intervention in matters that the shogunate had previously monopolized. In 1847 Kōmei exercised his religious authority by offering prayers to the gods at major shrines for the safety of the country.

THE COMING OF THE WEST

When U.S. commodore Matthew Perry and his "black ships" (two steam frigates and two sloops of war) entered Edo Bay on July 8, 1853, he confronted a government that, though financially weakened and riven by divisions, was fully aware of the threat posed by Western military technology.[7] Perry, who had been sent by President Millard Fillmore to establish relations with Japan, played to these fears by running out his cannon, refusing to allow curious onlookers to explore his ship, insisting that negotiations take place where he was, not in Nagasaki, and demanding that the shogun accept a letter from President Fillmore addressed to the emperor (Document 4). The letter required a response; having surveyed the coastline, Perry left with a promise to return the next year with a larger squadron to receive Japan's reply.

Perry's arrival caused such consternation that the shogun's senior councilors decided that dealing with his demands was not a decision they could make alone. Instead, the chief councilor, Abe Masahiro, circulated the letters and asked for recommendations. Informed of Perry's visit three days after he left, the imperial court again ordered prayers for the country's safety at major shrines. Later that year, it informed the shogunate that the emperor's mind was troubled at the thought of barbarians on the sacred soil of his ancestors. Representing the hard-line exclusionist position, Tokugawa Nariaki, the lord of Mito, argued that Japan had to fight, lest the foreigners' evil ways, especially Christianity but also trade, seduce the common people (Document 5). In contrast, Ii Naosuke, another vassal daimyo, took a more pragmatic approach. He argued that it would not be hard for Japan to learn the secrets of Western military technology and navigation. Once it had acquired a navy, it could again limit contact with foreigners. Abe Masahiro agreed that the foreigners held the advantage. Rather than fight a battle Japan was bound to lose, better to wait until conditions favored victory.

The pragmatists won. When Perry returned with a larger squadron in 1854, there was much banqueting and giving of gifts, including a miniature steam locomotive and a working telegraph. On March 31, the shogunate signed the Treaty of Peace and Amity, also called the Treaty of Kanagawa, which opened two ports where American ships could obtain supplies of food, firewood, and coal and also allowed the United States to station a consul at one of these ports, the isolated hamlet of Shimoda. The shogun's negotiators succeeded in refusing trade relations, but a "most favored nation clause" was included in the treaty.[8] This meant that any treaty advantage acquired by another nation would automatically apply to the United States as well. It was not reciprocal: Treaty privileges granted by the United States to European nations did not accrue to Japan.

Commoners' reaction to Perry's arrival was a mixture of fear and fascination. Some flocked to Uraga Bay, where Perry had dropped anchor, to view the black ships; many more bought cheap prints that depicted the ships and the sailors. Never having seen Westerners before, some printmakers drew on Buddhist iconography to depict Perry as a fierce demon (Document 6). Quick to sense a business opportunity, peddlers sold trinkets to American sailors, while printmakers sold over one million images of the barbarians and their warships to appease commoners' curiosity. At the same time, rural entrepreneurs organized farmer militias to protect communities against domestic disorder and the foreign threat.

After European powers followed the United States' lead in signing friendship agreements with Japan, the Americans succeeded in getting a commercial treaty. Townsend Harris, a failed businessman with experience in Siam (Thailand), was appointed U.S. consul in Shimoda, a town he found sadly bereft of amenities and so far from Edo that communicating with the shogun's representatives was difficult. Stationed there in 1856, Harris did not receive permission to present his credentials to the shogun for more than a year. Traveling in the style of the biannual daimyo processions to the capital, Harris entered Edo on November 30, 1857. He was the first foreign ambassador to be received in person by the shogun (Document 7). After the formalities, Harris warned Japanese officials of the dangers they faced unless they opened Japan to diplomacy as practiced in the West. If they did not take advantage of the magnanimous offer made by the United States, Britain might send gunboats to do in Japan what it had done in China, most recently in the Arrow War that began in 1856.

The men who negotiated Japan's first commercial treaty, the Treaty of Amity and Commerce, signed on July 29, 1858 (Document 8), did not simply cave in to Harris's demands. Although they accepted his argument that Japan had to enter into diplomatic relations in good faith, they avoided some of the most onerous conditions that had been imposed on China. (China had to allow opium to be imported, foreigners to buy land, and Christians to proselytize outside the treaty ports.) Harris wanted U.S. citizens to have the right of unrestricted travel in the Japanese interior. He also wanted six ports and cities, including the imperial capital of Kyoto, to be opened to trade. In the end, he had to settle for five treaty ports, which would be opened gradually over a period of five years (later extended to ten), with foreigners restricted to specified areas around them. Kyoto would remain off-limits.[9] The Japanese negotiators accepted the principle of extraterritoriality—the notion that judges of their own nationality would try foreigners who committed crimes on Japanese soil, and the guilty would be put in prisons run by their countrymen. American goods imported into Japan received low tariffs; Japanese goods sent to the United States faced high ones. The lack of reciprocity in extraterritoriality and tariff protection marked this treaty as unequal.

CONTROVERSY AND PURGE

The officials who negotiated the commercial treaty with Harris had to weather a firestorm of criticism. Even though leading daimyo understood that the new diplomatic relations were unavoidable, they worried that the simple act of negotiation had made Japan look weak. Starting with Tokugawa Nariaki, leaders urged the shogunate to strengthen its rule by appointing a capable man as the next shogun. Talent and ability, not hereditary rank, ought to become the primary criteria for office. In this way, treaty negotiations became embroiled in succession issues and proposals for reform, but worse was to come.

In an effort to unite the daimyo behind the commercial treaty, in 1858 the shogun's chief senior councilor, Hotta Masayoshi, decided that imperial sanction was needed. He even went to Kyoto to cajole the emperor into accepting the inevitable, arguing that the alternative would be an unwinnable war. Alas, the emperor refused to go along: "He [the emperor] greatly fears that to revolutionize the sound laws handed down from the time of Ieyasu would disturb the ideas of our people and make it impossible to preserve lasting tranquility." The treaty threatened "national honor" and "would endanger the national prestige."[10] News that the emperor opposed the treaty spread across Japan. By seeking approval for its dealings with foreigners, an approval it had never previously needed, the shogunate opened a new public sphere in which matters relating to national affairs could be debated in the name of the emperor.

The court of public opinion had opened as soon as the shogunate asked the daimyo what to do about Perry's demands; by the late 1850s it expanded through correspondence and broadsheets to encompass proposals for domestic reform as well. Even commoners submitted petitions to their lords with plans for resisting the foreign threat. *Sonnō-jōi*—"revere the emperor and expel the barbarians"—became the slogan of the day. Ruled by an outside daimyo, the southwestern domain of Chōshū was home to a notable number of radicals, later leaders of the Meiji government, who studied with Yoshida Shōin. In hopes of learning from the West, Shōin tried to get Perry to take him to America in 1854. Captured and turned over to the shogunate, he harangued his jailors on the proper relationship between emperor and subject. Back in Chōshū under house arrest, he ran a school that called for military reform and loyalty to the emperor. Following the signing of the Treaty of Amity and Commerce in 1858, he plotted to assassinate one of the shogun's ministers. He ended up in an Edo jail, where he wrote letters calling for a grassroots rebellion to restore the emperor to direct rule (Document 10).

Confronted by a barrage of criticism, the shogunate reasserted its authority. The new chief councilor, Ii Naosuke, accommodated the foreigners while leading the conservative opposition to the shogunate's critics. He selected the man with the better bloodline, not the greater talent, to be the next shogun; he ordered Tokugawa Nariaki and other daimyo who had opposed the treaty into house arrest; he browbeat the imperial court into acquiescing to the treaties signed not only with the

United States but with other nations that followed the U.S. lead, provided a means be found to expel the barbarians as soon as possible; and he beheaded men such as Yoshida Shōin who had challenged the established order (rather than allowing them an honorable death in suicide).

Although Ii used the purge of 1859 to silence his critics, he could not control people outside the ruling class. Tokugawa Nariaki had garnered favorable publicity for his opposition to the treaties. He was also seen as an able and intelligent daimyo who set an example of frugality and diligence. For him to be banished from Edo indicated that shogunal officials put their own interests ahead of the country's good. Acting on this understanding, a female schoolteacher and prophet from Mito, Kurosawa Tokiko, traveled to the imperial court in Kyoto with a petition — in the form of a long poem — that called for Nariaki's release and reinstatement (Document 9). A Shinto priest from Kurume, in Kyushu, went even further. Maki Izumi wrote a polemic calling on the emperor to lead an army to overthrow the shogun, execute Ii Naosuke and other traitors to the throne, and restore direct rule (Document 11).

On the snowy morning of March 24, 1860, samurai from Mito and Satsuma assassinated Ii Naosuke just outside the shogun's palace. This was the first time a minister had been assassinated since the seventeenth century, and that had been a private vendetta. Ii's assassins acted because in their eyes he had insulted the emperor, endangered Japan's national spiritual well-being, and amassed too much power. They did not want to destroy the shogunate; they simply wanted to return it to its proper function of respecting the emperor and suppressing barbarians (Document 12). Reports of what had happened attracted sightseers to the scene of the carnage, and private channels of information spread the news across the country. In modern times, the incident became a favorite of printmakers (Document 13), novelists, filmmakers, and television programmers for its example of selfless heroic action.

NEW POLICIES AND POLITICAL ALIGNMENTS

Ii's assassination exposed the dangers of allowing a split between emperor and shogun at a time when the crisis in foreign affairs demanded unity. It also emboldened opponents of conciliation with foreigners, who killed men such as Townsend Harris's translator and attacked the British legation in Edo. In the early 1860s, officials from Chōshū and Satsuma urged the court to demand a greater voice for itself and leading daimyo, as well as pardon for men punished by Ii and stiff penalties for his supporters. Cooperation was to be the new watchword, a policy supported even by shogunal officials who resented Ii's high-handedness.

Shortly after Ii's assassination, the new chief senior councilor proposed a royal wedding between Shogun Iemochi and the emperor's half-sister Princess Kazunomiya to demonstrate the unity between court and military. Both sides hoped to use the other. The shogun's men wanted to shore up the shogunate's prestige. Court nobles hoped that tying the marriage to a demand that foreigners be expelled would give the emperor control over national policy. In the end, the court was forced to recognize that Japan did not then have the military might to get rid of foreigners, but it extracted a promise that this desirable event would come soon. Kazunomiya dreaded leaving the city of her ancestors for the faraway military capital, but when the emperor threatened to abdicate, she gave in. Knowing of her reluctance, critics viewed the marriage as another sign of the shogun's disrespect for the emperor.

Not all samurai agreed with the emperor's desire that the shogunate return Japan to the conditions that had prevailed before Perry's arrival. Some advocated learning from the West by opening Japan and sending scholars abroad. One of them was Yokoi Shōnan, born in Kumamoto, in Kyushu, and educated in Edo, where he became friends with members of the Mito School and later adviser to Matsudaira Yoshinaga, the lord of the Fukui domain. Yokoi's 1860 treatise "The Three Major Problems of State Policy" echoed Aizawa's 1825 *New Theses* by urging the establishment of a state religion that could compete with Christianity, but he also argued that Japan had to develop its economy through foreign trade in order to build up its military (Document 14). He placed particular importance on a navy rather than coastal defense. In addition, he stressed the importance of government based on popular will, referring to Britain and America as models for political reform. His call for a rich country and strong military later became the slogan of the Meiji government.

Like Yokoi, a number of men understood that the current system of government was outmoded. In 1862 the shogunate carried out a series of measures called the Bunkyū era (1861–1863) reforms that reduced the shogun from undisputed hegemon to a contender for the role of determining the direction of foreign and domestic policy. Shogun Iemochi had already accepted the appointment of Matsudaira Yoshinaga as supreme councilor and Hitotsubashi Yoshinobu, his erstwhile rival in the 1858 shogunal succession dispute, as his guardian with the power to sanction all of his decisions. Reforms in the system of biannual attendance at the shogun's palace meant that the daimyo would no longer have to spend half their time in Edo; the money thus saved was to be devoted to military defense. For their families, this meant leaving Edo, where they had been forced to reside as hostages and returning to an unfamiliar homeland. In contrast to the Tenpō reforms, which had targeted the commoners' customary practices, the Bunkyū reforms focused more on administrative, fiscal, and military matters (Document 15).

In hindsight, the Bunkyū reforms marked the beginning of the end for the Tokugawa shogunate. Starting in 1859, a bustling foreign settlement had grown up in Yokohama, which soon became Japan's chief treaty port, attracting merchants and tourists. The foreigners chafed at the restrictions on travel imposed by the 1858 commercial treaty. On September 14, 1862, four British citizens on horseback crossed the path of the Satsuma regent. When the British refused to dismount or get out of the way, the regent's men killed one of them, a Shanghai-based merchant named Charles Richardson. The British government demanded that the perpetrators be brought to justice and an indemnity be paid to compensate the dead man's family. Believing himself to be in the right, the Satsuma regent refused, and the shogunate proved powerless to enforce compliance. Only an attack by British ships on the Satsuma capital of Kagoshima in August 1863 forced the domain to capitulate. Many Edo commoners saw that the government was not doing its job either internally or externally, and printmakers reflected their frustration (Document 16).

RECENTERING KYOTO

The first attempt to unify court and military failed to strengthen Edo's position in foreign and domestic matters. In the spring of 1863, the shogunate tried another strategy. Tokugawa Iemochi traveled to Kyoto in a grand procession of lords and retainers, the first time in 230 years that a shogun had visited the imperial capital. The plan was to awe the court, but once in Kyoto, the shogun faced humiliation at every turn. In the end, he was told that he had to live up to his earlier promise to "expel the barbarians." A date was set: June 25, 1863. He knew it was a promise he could not keep.

The shogun and activist daimyo were not the only arrivals to Kyoto in the early 1860s. Concern for the emperor's well-being led young samurai to abscond from their domains to get closer to the scene of action. Called *shishi* (men of high purpose), they thronged Kyoto's narrow streets, fastened on rumor as fact, and talked endlessly of how to ease the emperor's mind. In a reign of terror, they assassinated the servants of men who in their eyes had shown disrespect for the emperor and then threw body parts into the compounds of the shogun's advisers and cautious nobles as a warning to mend their ways. On April 9, 1863, just before the shogun arrived in Kyoto, nine scholars of Japan's ancient history decapitated the statues of the first three Ashikaga shoguns, who had betrayed the emperor five hundred years earlier. They then displayed the heads at a major river crossing with a manifesto promising the same punishment for contemporary traitors to the throne (Document 17).

The shogun was not amused. Although the assassins got away with murder, the men who had decapitated the statues were rounded up and threatened with execution. Among their supporters was a woman, Matsuo Taseko, who had left her village in Japan's central mountains to visit Kyoto, where she wrote poetry and mingled with the *shishi*. Fearing that she might be arrested, she found sanctuary in the Chōshū domain compound before escaping back home. There she wrote a long poem lamenting her weak woman's body, which implicitly lamented the inability of her comrades to act righteously on behalf of the emperor (Document 18).

Others took direct action. With the assistance of men from Satsuma, Matsudaira Katamori, daimyo of Aizu and one of the shogunate's staunchest supporters, drove the *shishi* affiliated with Chōshū out of Kyoto in September 1863. This spread unrest to the countryside, where the *shishi* rallied farmers to the imperial cause in two separate incidents. In the summer of 1864, three-sided factional fighting in Mito erupted into civil war. Remnants of the loyalist side fled across central Japan toward Kyoto, causing turmoil as they went. In the end, over fifteen hundred men died, and the resulting bitterness kept Mito sidelined for the remainder of the period. Meanwhile, in August 1864, Chōshū *shishi* tried to stage a comeback by invading Kyoto with the aim of rescuing the emperor from the men they believed were holding him prisoner. Both sides used arson as a weapon, a traditional battle tactic that caused grave damage to the city (Documents 19 and 20). The defeated forces, along with seven radical nobles, fled to Chōshū. Twice, once in 1864 and again in 1865, the shogunate launched punitive expeditions against the domain. The first saw Chōshū capitulate; the second, which appeared to threaten not just Chōshū but other domains' newfound opportunities to have a voice in foreign affairs, turned into a disaster for the shogunate. An anonymous commoner expressed his frustration with the shogun's ineptitude, as well as his fear of what the future might bring, in a satirical song (Document 21).

While the shogunate was trying to placate the emperor and leading daimyo, it also had to deal with disgruntled commoners. The opening of

Japan to foreign trade played havoc with the domestic economy. Some merchants prospered; Kyoto weavers discovered that the export market in silk reduced their supplies and drove up prices. Inflation was exacerbated by a breakdown in Japan's monetary system. Exposure to the international market revealed that gold was cheaper in Japan than it was elsewhere, resulting in the massive outflow of gold and the upending of the gold-copper ratio, to the detriment of commoners, whose daily transactions were denominated in copper. Bad weather and crop failures also contributed to social and economic instability. In Edo, townspeople accused merchants of hoarding, and in 1866 they punished the merchants by smashing up stores and trampling rice in the mud (Document 22). Large-scale uprisings with participants numbering in the thousands erupted with particular frequency in the months during which the shogunate was orchestrating military operations against Chōshū and in regions where it had administrative responsibility. Beginning on July 24, 1866, a violent outburst in the hinterland north of Edo swept up over 100,000 men, women, and children and spread across several provinces (Document 23). Although the participants demanded justice, not regime change, their actions reflected badly on the shogunate's ability to maintain order.

FALL OF THE SHOGUNATE

Having failed at conciliating the emperor and leading daimyo, Tokugawa officials decided that their best hope was to strengthen shogunal authority at everyone else's expense. Many men found it difficult to go beyond some modification of the existing arrangements; even if the emperor were to be restored to some semblance of direct rule, losing his military advisers was unthinkable. Others wanted a return to the ancient form of government that had existed in the eighth century. Daimyo and their advisers proposed new forms of government that would open policymaking to men beyond the shogun's advisory council and provide opportunities for them to exercise their talent and ability on behalf of emperor and nation. The wide range of proposals that surfaced shows that many men pondered how to organize a government and what its purpose should be. It also suggests that the regime that finally emerged in the 1870s was not the inevitable result of a predetermined path; other options existed.

Generally speaking, reformers proposed either broadening the political arena to be more inclusive or concentrating power in a strong leader. In 1866 a leading proponent of westernization, Fukuzawa Yukichi, drew on his understanding of events taking place in Europe to advocate a more absolutist form of government in which authority would be centralized under the aegis of the shogun (Document 24). In late 1867, shortly before being assassinated for having brought the southwestern domains of Chōshū and Satsuma together to overthrow the shogunate, Sakamoto Ryōma, a low-ranking samurai from Tosa, proposed that a system of elections replace appointment to office by hereditary right (Document 25). The shogunal official Katsu Kaishū proposed a national assembly that would share power between officials from the shogunate, the domains, and the imperial court. Just before the outbreak of civil war in 1868, Katsu wrote an irate letter to his colleagues that criticized them for their selfish concerns rather than considering the good of the nation as a whole. Unlike most officials, he placed his hopes in the commoners, whose intelligence and knowledge had increased since the country had opened to foreign trade (Document 29).

From August through January 1868, a series of popular movements with remarkably mixed messages swept Japan from Hiroshima in the west to Yokohama in the east. First paper talismans and then coins, masks, and sacred objects such as wooden grave tablets fell from the sky (some said instigated by secret agents from Chōshū). Seeing these as gifts from heaven that foretold a bountiful new world, crowds danced in the streets, chanting *"Ee ja nai ka"* (Ain't it great). In some cases, the crowds celebrated a bountiful harvest after the miserable one the preceding year; others looked forward to the opening of another treaty port at Hyōgo (now Kobe) (Document 26). In the village of Fujisawa, near Yokohama, the participants threw stones at foreigners in a gesture that mimicked driving out devils. They even fashioned a coffin and held a mock funeral for the shogunate (Document 27).

The shogunate was in trouble. When Shogun Iemochi died in 1866 (he was only twenty years old), Hitotsubashi Yoshinobu, his rival in 1858, replaced him and took the Tokugawa name. Emperor Kōmei (he was thirty-six) died the following year. Although he opposed signing treaties with foreigners and saw expulsion as his sacred duty, he supported the existing arrangement whereby the shogun ruled on his behalf. For people who wanted to restore the emperor to direct rule, his death was so fortuitous that rumors of poison spread. Ensconced in the shogun's palace in Kyoto, Yoshinobu realized that he no longer commanded the allegiance of his relatives or many of his vassal daimyo, let alone the outside daimyo. Hoping that a graceful exit would preserve Tokugawa dominance in policy-making circles, owing to the shogunate's economic clout as the largest single domain in Japan, he resigned as shogun in November 1867 and withdrew to Osaka (Document 28).

REGIME CHANGE

The new regime was born in blood, its future far from certain. Yoshinobu's abrupt resignation left a power vacuum in Kyoto, which activist court nobles and outside daimyo from the southwestern domains filled. Yoshinobu decided to respond by marching his army back toward Kyoto on January 27, 1868. Armed with modern weapons bought from the West, and with samurai leading troops made up of well-disciplined commoners, his enemies ambushed the Tokugawa forces and dealt them a stinging defeat at Toba-Fushimi. Yoshinobu was immediately branded an "enemy of the court." Named after the sexagenary cycle year in which it began (the year of the *boshin*, or earth dragon), the Boshin Civil War of 1868–1869 had begun (Map 2).

Although Yoshinobu took no part in the fighting, his allies in northeastern Japan put up fierce resistance to the armies that marched in the emperor's name (largely composed of troops from Satsuma and Chōshū, supplemented by *shishi* from other parts of Japan). They fought less to restore the Tokugawa shogunate than out of regional antipathy to the southwestern domains, which they accused of selfishly plotting to establish a new shogunate that would serve regional interests. Edo's flammable houses were spared the fate of Kyoto in 1864 (Document 20) when on April 5–6 the shogun's representative, Katsu Kaishū, negotiated terms of surrender with Satsuma's Saigō Takamori. As a result, on May 3 the imperial forces entered Edo Castle. The last person to leave the site from which the Tokugawa shoguns had ruled Japan for over 260 years was Tenshō-in, the widow of the thirteenth shogun and originally from Satsuma. Commoners admired her fidelity, and as one satirical poem suggests, they were already disenchanted with their new rulers (Document 30). One group of Tokugawa loyalists resisted surrender. They made camp at the shogun's mausoleum on Ueno Hill, where they defied the new regime with guerrilla attacks for another two months before being routed on July 4, 1868. Meanwhile, the imperial banner marched north, to the strains of a new song that demanded universal reverence for the emperor (Document 31).

Sendai led an alliance of thirty-one domains, called the Northeastern League, with the aim of putting a different prince on the throne. It did not hold together for long. First Akita, home to scholars who supported direct rule by the emperor, and then other domains defected to the imperial side. In possession of superior weaponry, including Armstrong guns (artillery), minié rifles, and Spencer repeating rifles, the imperial army pounded the "rebels" into submission one by one. The fiercest battles erupted in Aizu, home to Matsudaira Katamori, who had earned the enmity

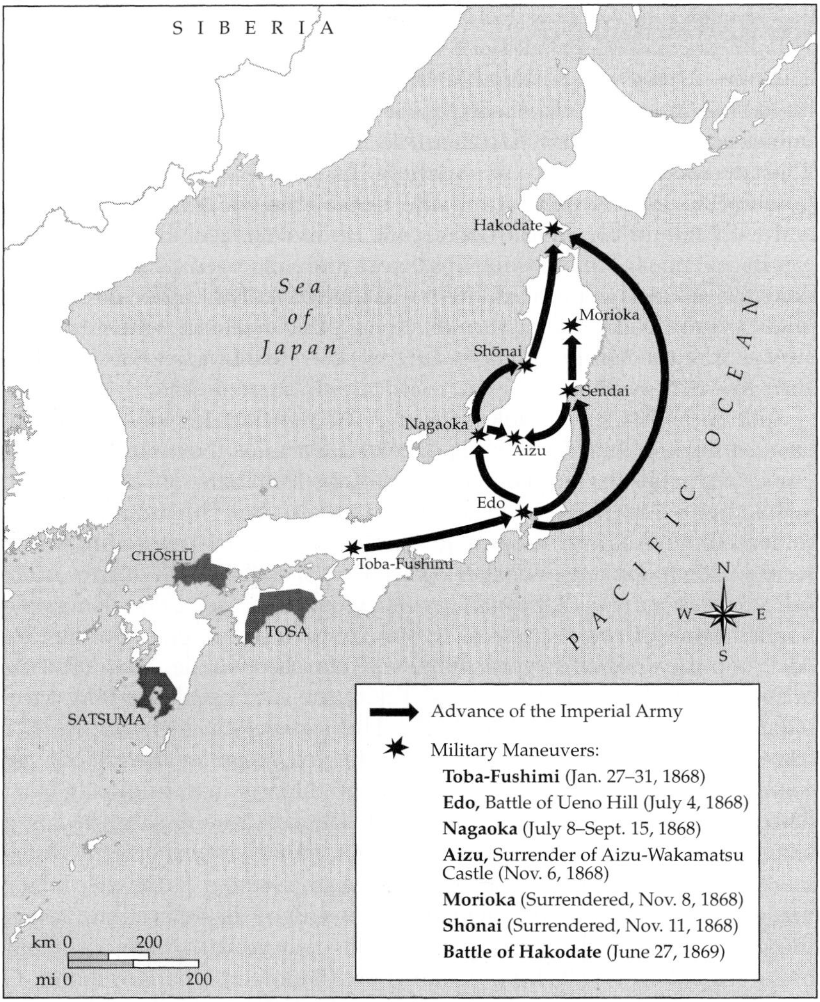
SIBERIA
Sea of Japan
PACIFIC OCEAN
Hakodate
Morioka
Shōnai
Sendai
Nagaoka
Aizu
Edo
Toba-Fushimi
CHŌSHŪ
TOSA
SATSUMA
N
W
E
S
km 0 200
mi 0 200
Advance of the Imperial Army
Military Maneuvers:
Toba-Fushimi (Jan. 27–31, 1868)
Edo, Battle of Ueno Hill (July 4, 1868)
Nagaoka (July 8–Sept. 15, 1868)
Aizu, Surrender of Aizu-Wakamatsu Castle (Nov. 6, 1868)
Morioka (Surrendered, Nov. 8, 1868)
Shōnai (Surrendered, Nov. 11, 1868)
Battle of Hakodate (June 27, 1869)

Map 2. *Boshin Civil War, 1868–1869*

of Chōshū and later Satsuma for his able defense of Tokugawa interests as military governor of Kyoto. Aizu warriors fought for honor; their
women joined them in the castle, confronted muzzle-loading rifles with
halberds, and found other ways to support their menfolk (Document 32).
Fearing that the battle had already been lost, the White Tiger Troop of
teenage boys committed mass suicide on a hill overlooking the castle.
Aizu lost more men than any other domain. It also received the harsh-
est punishment: Its retainers were moved to a barren strip of land and
told to become farmers, and Katamori was deprived of all honors and
made a Shinto priest. Even Tokugawa Yoshinobu was forced to do no
more than retire as head of the Tokugawa family. After the surrender of
Aizu-Wakamatsu Castle on November 7, 1868, the Northeastern League
quickly disintegrated, but the end of the Boshin Civil War came only in
June 1869 with the surrender of Tokugawa naval officers under the command of Enomoto Takeaki, who had established the Republic of Ezo at
Hakodate, in Hokkaido.

Historians give various reasons for why the shogunate collapsed and
the southwestern domains won. By the middle of the nineteenth century,
the mismatch between wealth and power was obvious to members of the
ruling class and commoners alike. Far from being the "stupid people"
castigated by Aizawa, commoners had a shrewd understanding of their
political betters, and they were not impressed. On the one hand, they
wanted a stable regime to protect their livelihoods; on the other, they
desired the freedom to do what they wanted. Confronted with Western
pressure to open Japan to trade, the shogunate was unable to negotiate
without pulling other political actors into the picture. But the shogunate's
weakness tells only part of the story. While all sides tried to acquire the
latest in Western weapons, thanks to earlier reforms, Chōshū had the
deeper pockets and more rigorous training program. Once the southwestern domains had overcome internal rivalries and had the emperor
in their power, they used his name to rally other domains to their side.
Some domains hesitated to attack the imperial banner out of loyalty to
the emperor; others stayed on the sidelines either because they lacked
the financial resources to fight or because they did not want to give the
foreigners an excuse to meddle in Japan's internal affairs.

NATIONAL CONSOLIDATION

Carrying out national consolidation required more than winning battles.
While the fight against "enemies of the court" was under way, on April 6,
1868, the sixteen-year-old emperor offered a pledge to his imperial ancestors

stating the principles that were to inform the new government. Officially called the Charter Oath (Document 33), this set of five articles promised that his administration would listen to a wide range of opinions, establish national unity, seek knowledge from throughout the world, and give people the freedom to fulfill their aspirations, thereby ending hereditary status restrictions. The next day, signboards appeared throughout the country announcing that the emperor would rule Japan directly and that his government would enforce the international treaties previously signed by representatives of the shogunate. The injunctions also ordered people to help one another, refrain from violence and needless "wandering," and obey orders.

The new government faced myriad challenges, not least of which was its lack of resources. It solicited contributions from wealthy farmers and merchants to fight the Boshin Civil War, but ad hoc donations could not fund ongoing expenditures. Although it moved swiftly to confiscate most of the Tokugawa dominion, daimyo who had not fought on the losing side continued to rule their domains. This deprived the center of tax receipts and of control over large portions of Japan's inhabitants, most of whom felt greater loyalty to their village or lord than to a faraway emperor. To give the new government credibility, on March 5, 1869, daimyo from the southwestern domains made a show of returning the population and land registers that confirmed their authority over their domains to the imperial government, the idea being that in accordance with ancient principle, Japan belonged to the emperor. The other daimyo soon followed suit. Before they took such a drastic step, they received an understanding that the emperor would confirm their rights. Instead of lordly titles, they were now to be known as domain governors. Their retainers, too, became public officials, although the central government had no control over them.

The new system proved unworkable. The domain governors and their officials put their domains' interests above the center. They competed in attracting trade, and they ignored the central government's directives. In short, they continued to act independently. In addition, there were far too many of them; a country as small as Japan did not need a multitude of autonomous administrative units. In 1871, both to make administration more efficient and to counteract the tendency of local officials to go their own way, Kido Takayoshi, from Chōshū, took the lead in proposing to do away with the domains and establish seventy-two prefectures, with later reductions in number to come (Document 34). The Meiji government bought off the daimyo with promises of high rank in the new combined court-military nobility and generous government-paid stipends. It took over the domain debts that had bedeviled the daimyo for generations, and except for personal staffs, it took responsibility for retainers. Each samurai received a stipend (later commuted to a lump sum), encouragement to find some other line of work, and the legal designation of "former samurai" to distinguish the samurai from commoners. Although much remained to be done in terms of institution building, the abolition of domains and the establishment of prefectures meant that by 1872 the old military regime was dead.

On December 23, 1871, most of the leadership, having taken the first steps to create a centralized national government, departed Japan for the United States and Europe, leaving behind a caretaker regime. Named for the court noble Iwakura Tomomi, the mission included Kido Takayoshi, the architect of the plan to establish prefectures; Ōkubo Toshimichi, the representative from Satsuma; and Itō Hirobumi, who later drafted the Meiji Constitution. A number of former shogunal officials joined the mission as translators and secretaries, and five girls—one of whom, Tsuda Umeko, was only seven years old—accompanied it to the United States, where they were going to study. The mission hoped to revise the unequal treaties signed by the shogunate, but it soon realized that Japan would have to reform its own legal system for this to become possible. Instead, the mission's members devoted themselves to investigating the secrets of the West's strength. They visited factories, questioned legal scholars, spoke with mayors, and viewed with astonishment the courtesy with which Western men treated their womenfolk. They also saw, below the sheen of civilization, the wretched lives of industrial workers and people displaced by machines. During the 631 days of their trip, they came to realize that Japan, too, could acquire modern scientific knowledge, and it could build the machines that powered the industrial revolution. A speech given in English by Itō Hirobumi to an audience in San Francisco on January 18, 1872, disclosed a Japan ready to join the fellowship of nations and a Japan determined to make its mark on the world (Document 35).

THE MEIJI RESTORATION IN WORLD HISTORY

Historians have long debated how to define the Meiji Restoration. The era (1868–1912) takes its name from the Meiji emperor: 1868 was the year he was restored to the direct rule that his ancestors had last enjoyed in the eighth century (if then). The emperor, however, did not hold the reins of power. Because the men who engineered his ascent were themselves

members of the ruling class, and because the war that followed the shogun's resignation lasted just over a year, some historians have deemed
this regime change nothing more than a coup d'état—the replacement
of one set of rulers with another. Others have argued that the economic,
social, and cultural changes occurring during the course of the nineteenth
century simply intensified after 1868, making the restoration no more than
a transition from one political system to another. Still others have empha-
sized the extraordinary differences between Japan in 1800 and Japan in
1900 by calling this the Meiji *transformation*. And some prefer the term
revolution because it emphasizes the new ways of thinking and acting in
political, social, economic, and cultural terms brought about by the process of national consolidation.

Calling Japan's mid-nineteenth-century transformation a *restoration*
obscures the processes that brought it about and their parallels around
the world. Many of the documents in this volume display a devotion and
loyalty to Japan that are characteristic of nineteenth-century nationalism
in general. As in France and other European countries, a consciousness
of a shared land, language, history, and religion motivated Japanese government leaders and activists to seek ways to strengthen the nation against
outside threats.

Efforts by these leaders to first try reform, for fear of instability and
foreign interference, paralleled initiatives in other parts of the world.
Multiethnic empires such as the Ottoman Empire, Russia, and China,
for example, used this means to deal with domestic disorder and external pressure. Nineteenth-century Ottoman sultans aimed at reforming
the military and then the bureaucracy, but the rising tide of nationalism
in outlying provinces in the Balkans and North Africa, abetted by Russia
and the European powers, increasingly threatened their rule. Reforms
in China following the Opium War were hampered by rapacious foreign
demands, a devastating political and religious upheaval known as the Taiping Rebellion (1850–1864), and a growing divide between the Manchu
court in Beijing and ethnic Chinese (Han) officials. When Britain defeated
Russia in the Crimean War (1853–1856), the Russian tsar reformed the
army, the legal system, education, and local government; he also eman-
cipated the serfs. His actions pleased neither the landed aristocracy nor
urban intellectuals, and he was assassinated in 1881. Ethnically homogeneous nations fared better. Britain initiated a series of reforms that
gave more men political participation and a sense of shared purpose.

Japan had the advantage in that it could tie reform to nationalism as
Britain did, but in the end reform was not enough. To strengthen the
nation against outside threats required the construction of a more unified

nation-state than had existed in the past, in conformity with a global pattern of national consolidation. For the same reason and based on the same nationalist principles of common language and culture, Germany and Italy pulled nations out of formerly contending states. In the Western Hemisphere, Canada achieved independence from Britain as a unified dominion; the Civil War in the United States ended with enhanced central authority over the states and a renewed sense of national pride. In short, the Meiji Restoration fits well within worldwide trends toward national integration and unification.

NOTES

[1]For general information on Japan's premodern economic development, see Akira Hayami, Osamu Saito, and Ronald P. Toby, eds., *Emergence of Economic Society in Japan, 1600–1859* (Oxford: Oxford University Press, 2004).

[2]Constantine Vaporis shows how a "culture of movement" developed in the late eighteenth and early nineteenth centuries, based on substantial travel for leisure as well as business. See *Breaking Barriers: Travel and the State in Early Modern Japan* (Cambridge Mass.: Council on East Asian Studies, Harvard University, 1994).

[3]Tokugawa Ieyasu claimed that he governed the realm as Japan's public authority. Early-nineteenth-century scholars of Japan's ancient past took the term *bakufu* ("tent government," which designated the offices under a commander in the field) from Chinese history and applied it to the Tokugawa military regime to emphasize its transient nature, in contrast to the eternal imperial court. The term has been used by historians ever since.

[4]Gilbert Rozman, "Social Change," in *The Cambridge History of Japan*, vol. 5, *The Nineteenth Century*, ed. Marius B. Jansen (Cambridge: Cambridge University Press, 1989), 547–48.

[5]David Howell, "Foreign Encounters and Informal Diplomacy in Early Modern Japan," *Journal of Japanese Studies* 40, no. 2 (Summer 2014): 295–327.

[6]Bob Tadashi Wakabayashi, *Anti-Foreignism and Western Learning in Early-Modern Japan: The New Theses of 1825* (Cambridge, Mass.: Council on East Asian Studies, Harvard University, 1991), 60.

[7]John W. Dower, "Black Ships & Samurai," MIT Visualizing Cultures, http://ocw.mit.edu/ans7870/21f/21f.027/black_ships_and_samurai/bss_essay01.html.

[8]For the text of the Treaty of Peace and Amity between the United States of America and Japan, also known as the Treaty of Kanagawa, see https://www.archives.gov/exhibits/featured_documents/treaty_of_kanagawa/treaty_images.html.

[9]Michael R. Auslin, *Negotiating with Imperialism: The Unequal Treaties and the Culture of Japanese Diplomacy* (Cambridge, Mass.: Harvard University Press, 2004).

[10]W. G. Beasley, trans. and ed., *Select Documents on Japanese Foreign Policy, 1853–1868* (London: Oxford University Press, 1955), 181.

PART TWO

The Documents

1

Setting the Scene: External Pressure and Domestic Turmoil

1

AIZAWA SEISHISAI

New Theses

1825

Aizawa Seishisai (1782–1863) was an early advocate of the policy of sonnō-jōi— "revere the emperor and expel the barbarians"—and a leading scholar of the Mito School of historical studies, which provided intellectual support for the restoration of imperial rule. Beginning in the 1790s, foreign ships from Russia, Britain, and the United States made several attempts to call at Japanese ports other than Nagasaki, where the Dutch were allowed to trade. Aizawa completed his New Theses *(Shinron) in 1825, soon after the Tokugawa shogunate issued an edict demanding that all foreign ships (except those under the Dutch flag) be fired on "without a second thought." According to Aizawa, countering the foreign threat required more than military readiness. He stressed the need for moral and spiritual armament, fearing that wily foreigners would capture the hearts and minds of Japanese commoners. National unity depended on the propagation of a national religion that could counter the pernicious appeal of Christianity. Aizawa sought to popularize the sacred nature of the Japanese state (kokutai), rightly ruled over by emperors*

Bob Tadashi Wakabayashi, *Anti-Foreignism and Western Learning in Early-Modern Japan: The* New Theses *of 1825* (Cambridge, Mass.: Council on East Asian Studies, Harvard University, 1986), 149–50, 152, 158, 163–64, 167–70.

who were descendants of the Japanese gods and destined one day to rule over the entire world. Aizawa's New Theses is often referred to as the bible of the leaders of the Meiji Restoration. It proved equally inspirational for nationalistic thinkers well into the twentieth century.

Prefatory Remarks

Our Divine Realm is where the sun emerges. It is the source of the primordial vital force sustaining all life and order. Our Emperors, descendants of the Sun Goddess, Amaterasu, have acceded to the Imperial Throne in each and every generation, a unique fact that will never change. Our Divine Realm rightly constitutes the head and shoulders of the world and controls all nations. It is only proper that our Divine Realm illuminates the entire universe and that our dynasty's sphere of moral suasion knows no bounds. But recently the loathsome Western barbarians, unmindful of their base position as the lower extremities of the world, have been scurrying impudently across the Four Seas, trampling other nations under foot. Now they are audacious enough to challenge our exalted position in the world. What manner of insolence is this?

> (Gloss:[1] The earth lies amid the heavenly firmament, is round in shape, and has no edges. All things exist as nature dictates. Thus, our Divine Realm is at the top of the world. Though not a very large country, it reigns over the Four Quarters because its Imperial Line has never known dynastic change. The Western barbarians represent the thighs, legs, and feet of the universe. This is why they sail hither and yon, indifferent to the distances involved. Moreover, the country they call America is located at the rear end of the world, so its inhabitants are stupid and incompetent. All of this is as nature dictates.)

These barbarians court ultimate ruin by ignoring the moral laws of nature and refusing to accept the lowliness of their status. But alas, the normative forces of Heaven and Earth must wane as well as wax: "When the power of men is immense, they overcome Heaven." Unless a Great Hero bestirs himself to assist Heaven's normative processes, all creation will fall prey to the wily, meat-eating [uncivilized] barbarians.

Yet today, when I propose great plans to benefit the realm, people look at one another in astonishment; they are all taken aback. This is because they cling to conventional ideas and to outmoded, inaccurate

---

[1]These glosses were provided in the original *New Theses*.

sources of information [about foreign countries]. *Sun Tzu* says, "Do not rely on the enemy's staying away; be ever prepared to keep him away. Do not rely on his not attacking; make yourself immune to any attack." If we govern and edify well, if we make the people's morals pure and their customs beautiful, if we induce high and low alike to embody righteousness, if we enrich the people and strengthen our arms, if we make ourselves immune to attack from even the strongest of enemies, all will be well. But if we neglect these tasks, if we are complacent and lax, what is there for us to rely on?

But skeptics argue, "They are only barbarians in merchant ships and fishing boats. They pose no serious problem; there is no grave danger." Such skeptics rely on the barbarians' staying away, on their not attacking; they rely on something not within our power to control. Should I question them about our military preparedness or immunity to attack, they would be dumbfounded. Ah, how can we prevent the world from falling prey to the barbarians? . . .

What Is Essential to a Nation

The ancient sage kings did not maintain the realm, prevent unrest, and uphold everlasting domestic tranquility by forcing their people into submission. Such methods may work for a single reign [but not forever]. Instead, the ancient sages relied on something else: "all people in the realm were of one heart and mind"; they were so endeared of their rulers that separation was unbearable. This is what we can really rely on.

Ever since earth became distinct from the firmament and men came into being, a Divine Line of Emperors descended from the Sun Goddess Amaterasu has ruled the realm. Can it be mere coincidence that no one has ever had evil designs on the throne? Loyalty of subject for ruler is the greatest moral precept of the cosmos. Affection between parent and child is the ultimate form of blessing within the realm. This greatest of moral precepts and this ultimate form of blessing exist together between Heaven and Earth; they slowly and steadily seep into men's hearts in all places and eras. By understanding and utilizing the sentiments of loyalty and filial devotion, the ancient sage kings regulated the realm and forever upheld nature's moral order among their people. . . .

When we recall how ancestors reverently served the progenitress of our Imperial Line and other Heavenly Deities, how can we ignore ancestral will? How can we turn against our ruler? Through such rituals, filial devotion is transmitted from father to son, and from son to grandson. Each carries on the wishes of his parent and bids his offspring to do likewise. The passing of a thousand generations produces not the slightest change in their filial sentiment. Loyalty and filial devotion have always been one and the same: Filial devotion is transformed into loyalty to ruler, and loyalty is demonstrated by respecting the wishes of forbears. Edification of the people and the reform of their folkways is accomplished: The ruler places the people under his "inducing influence" without recourse to injunctions or exhortations. Religious rituals are a means of political rule, and political rule is identical to ethical inculcation. Throughout history, edification and administration have been inseparable: When the people are taught simply to revere Amaterasu and Her Divine Imperial Line, the allegiances are undivided and they are blind to all heresies. Thus we achieve both spiritual unity among the people and the union of Heaven and man. This was the ancient sage kings' one true reliance for maintaining the realm, and was the basis on which Amaterasu founded our nation. . . .

But because peace has prevailed for so long, lassitude has set in. The typical daimyo today enjoys a life of ease and softness from birth. His lack of measures to deal with natural disasters causes him no concern. Renegades roam freely throughout his domain, but he takes no steps to outlaw them. Foreign barbarians reconnoiter our perimeter, but he pays them no heed. This amounts to forsaking the land and people placed in his charge. The typical retainer today thinks only of his own well-being, not of loyalty to domain or of solving problems on its behalf. He is lax and irresponsible, is a disgrace to his ancestors, and is unmindful of blessings received from his lord. When daimyo and retainer alike are this derelict in their duty, how can we unite the land and people? How can we maintain the spiritual solidarity that makes land and people a nation?

When a Great Hero seeks to rouse the realm to action, his only fear is that the people will not respond. But when leaders of mediocre talent temporize and gloss over problems, their only fear is that the people may indeed respond. Hence they patch up affairs to create an aura of normality and calm. They even allow foreigners to land on our shores, and afterward, in high and low places, cover up the truth by declaring that those barbarians were fishermen in search of provisions. Such [handling of this recent affair] betrays an attitude of minimizing the potential threat posed by the barbarians, an attitude which can only spell trouble. . . .

The ancient sages taught rulers the Way—how to cultivate themselves and rule over others—and nothing else. Scholars of late cannot understand this. On the one hand, perverse Confucians expound petty theories and distort the true meaning of the classics, trying to appear original or erudite. On the other, petty men of letters vie for fame and fortune. But such riff-raff are the least of our problems. The true source of our malaise lies in four other types of scholars. First there are those who designate the Ming and Qing, rather than our Divine Realm, "Middle Kingdom Civilization." They are ignorant of the virtue of name and status, and disgrace our nation. Second are those who, misled by short-term trends in our history, distort names and abandon virtue by depicting the Emperor as a defunct monarch in exile. This impairs the Imperial Line's transforming powers and defames the shogunate's virtuous achievements. Third are small-minded advocates of fiscal solvency and administrative efficiency who style themselves "political economists." Finally are those who expound concepts from Sung Learning, such as "nature" or "Heaven's Will," in seemingly impressive tones and with an imposing mien, but who really are sham Confucians, indifferent to the tasks of the day. None of these four types of scholars represent loyalty, filial devotion, and the Way of Yao, Shun, and Confucius.

In short, Amaterasu's moral precepts have been disrupted by shaman cultists, transformed into something alien by Buddhist clerics, and debased by perverse Confucians and petty men of letters. Because such wicked doctrines were so diverse and contradictory, they destroyed the people's spiritual unity [achieved in antiquity by Amaterasu]. Loyalty of subject for ruler and affection between parent and child are now utterly ignored, leading us to wonder if the Way of Heaven and Man really exists.

In times past, even the worst spreaders of sedition were fellow-nationals working from within. But the Western barbarians are different. They all believe in the same religion, Christianity, which they use to annex territories. Wherever they go, they destroy native houses of worship, deceive the local peoples, and seize those lands. These barbarians will settle for nothing less than subjugating the rulers of all nations and conscripting all peoples into their ranks. And they are becoming aggressive. Having overthrown the native regimes on Luzon and Java, they turned their predatory eyes on our Divine Realm. They instigated insurrections in Kyushu using the same methods as on Luzon and Java: Not only in Japan have nefarious commoners led people astray by spreading wicked doctrines. Fortunately, our enlightened lords and their astute advisors perceived the foreigners' pernicious designs and took steps to exterminate them. Due to our leaders' wise policies, Christianity was utterly eradicated. Not a single adherent remained alive to subvert our Middle Kingdom, and our people have been spared from the foreigners' wiles for two hundred years.

Even so, Amaterasu's Great Way is not fully elucidated, and the people have nothing to rely on spiritually. What is more, there are as many nefarious commoners in our midst as ever, and if they do not owe their allegiance to shamanism or Buddhism, then most surely they commit themselves to some perverse form of Confucianism or belletristic foolishness. Our present situation is like that of a patient recovering from a near-fatal disease: Though his life is no longer in danger, he is weak and in doubt about his best future course of action. He needs something spiritual to rely on within, and he is attracted to many harmful things from without.

One source of harm that has appeared of late is Dutch Studies. This discipline grew out of translation work — the reading and deciphering of Dutch books by specially trained interpreter-officials. There is no harm in Dutch Studies itself; the harm comes when some dupe with a smattering of second-hand knowledge of foreign affairs mistakenly lauds the far-fetched notions spun out by Western barbarians or publishes books to that effect in an attempt to transform our Middle Kingdom to barbarian ways. There are, moreover, many curiosities and concoctions from abroad that dazzle the eye and entice our people to glorify foreign ways. Should the wily barbarians someday be tempted to take advantage of this situation and entice our stupid commoners to adopt beliefs and customs that reek of barbarism, how could we stop them? [The *Book of Changes* tells us,] "The lining of frost on which we tread [in the early winter soon] turns into a hard sheet of ice." We must adopt appropriate measures to thwart them now, before it is too late.

Now, when barbarians prowl about our coasts harboring pernicious designs on us, wicked doctrines of all sorts are rife within. Nurturing barbarism within our Middle Kingdom will trigger disturbances, throughout the realm: Commoners will hatch evil conspiracies; and fawning men will collaborate. What would become of us? Would we still be the Middle Kingdom Civilization? Or would we be transformed into another Ming or Qing [China]? Or into an Indian [Buddha-Land]? Or into a Western [barbarian state]? Just what is essential for a land and people to be a nation (*kokutai*)? Without four limbs, a man is not a man. Similarly, a nation has some "requisite and defining entity" that makes it what it is. Some people stress the need to enrich our country and strengthen our arms in order to defend our borders. But the foreign beasts now seek to exploit the fact that people in outlying areas crave a source of spiritual reliance: They furtively beguile our commoners into betraying us. Should the barbarians win our people's hearts and minds, they will have captured the realm without a skirmish. Then the "wealth and strength" that these people stress would no longer be ours to employ. In effect, we would provide arms for the brigand and provisions for the bandit. What a pity, if, after all our meticulous planning and painstaking effort, we merely ended up joining the enemy's ranks! No one who understands such matters can help being angry and vexed.

The shogunate has decreed resolutely that all contact between commoners in outlying areas and barbarians is strictly forbidden, that commoners may not aid and abet barbarians. This is to prevent the wily foreign curs from luring our people into their fold. Because of this decree, everyone in the realm, wise and foolish alike, is aware of the foreign beasts' loathsome nature and of their detestable designs on us. This is the indomitable spirit of our people.

Though present and past be far removed, His Imperial Majesty is a Descendant of the same Dynastic Line founded by Amaterasu. The masses below are descendants of those masses first blessed by Amaterasu's loving grace in antiquity. If we establish a set of doctrines for the people in keeping with their indomitable spirit, if we serve Heaven, if we revere forbears, if we recompense Amaterasu's original gifts to us, if we remain true to our ancestors in the spirit that she displayed in caring for Her subjects long ago, and if we rectify the loyalty of subject for lord and make warmer still the affection between parent and child, then it will not be difficult to edify the people and achieve spiritual unity. An opportunity like this will not come again in a thousand years—we must exploit it!

2

ŌSHIO HEIHACHIRŌ

A Call to Arms

March 25, 1837

In the early nineteenth century, the Tokugawa leadership faced both foreign threats and domestic difficulties. The intrusion of a commercial economy into the countryside had explosive results. Peasant riots were sometimes directed against so-called evil officials who threatened the well-being of the entire village, but wealthy landlords within villages or

Michael Eastwood, trans., *Readings in Tokugawa Thought*, 3rd ed., Select Papers, Volume No. 9 (Chicago: The Center for East Asian Studies, University of Chicago, 1998), 183–86.

wealthy merchants in cities increasingly became the targets of riots. These incidents rose dramatically during the famine years of the 1830s.

The best known of these riots was the Osaka uprising of 1837, led by Ōshio Heihachirō (1793–1837), a police officer in Osaka and student of Wang Yangming, a Chinese thinker who stressed the unity of thought and action. Ōshio blamed the hard times on corrupt government officials and self-serving merchants. Burning with indignation, he issued the manifesto translated below urging "all the commoners throughout the world" to punish those who refused to aid the starving. Putting thought into action, on March 25, 1837, he led a band of angry farmers into the city and set fire to government offices and merchant warehouses. When his rebellion failed, Ōshio committed suicide, but his emotional call to action established a model for radical political deeds, evident first among the shishi *(men of high purpose) who rebelled against the Tokugawa regime in the 1860s and later among young military officers who sought to liberate the emperor from the control of capitalists and politicians in the 1930s.*

Received from Heaven itself
  To all the commoners throughout the world

"When throughout the four seas there is only suffering, the blessings of Heaven will be forever ended, and when petty men are allowed to govern the nation, catastrophes become commonplace." In this way the Ancient Sages firmly forewarned all succeeding generations of rulers and ministers of the people. Hence even the sacred founder of our regime [Ieyasu] embraced the extension of compassion to base people as the basis of benevolent government. However, during the 240–50 years of the Great Peace, the people above increasingly lived in openly arrogant corruption and took bribes, and by relying on secret connections with the women of the inner chambers, lowly men with neither the virtues of benevolence nor righteousness rose to positions of high power and devoted themselves only to schemes to enrich themselves and their houses. These daimyo and retainers imposed excessive taxes on all the farming people; these are inhuman orders to issue on top of the heavy suffering of the existing taxes and corvée. As the volume of taxation piled up, suffering spread throughout the four seas, and everyone, without exception, came to hate those who ruled. From Edo at the center, all of the domains fell into the practice of such deeds.

Since the rule of the Ashikaga house, the emperor has been kept apart as though in exile and lost the authority to prescribe rewards and punishments, and the commoners, having no place to direct their protests, saw that they had no recourse and degenerated into disorder. Their spirit of anger rose up to Heaven, and year by year earthquake, fire, and disaster made mountains crumble and floods arise. Moreover, all of these disasters flowed from Heaven, and ultimately the five grains were blighted and people starved. These were all serious admonishments from Heaven, which should be heeded, but all those above paid no attention. The wicked ranks of men carried out important policies, fatiguing the polity, and schemed together to take money and rice. For that reason we who hide in the shadows of the grass sense the situation, but having neither the authority of the great kings Tang and Wu, nor the morality of Confucius or Mencius, we idly remained uninvolved.

During the recent upsurge in rice prices the Commissioner of Osaka as well as all the administrators ignored the benevolence that pervades all things. They carried out arbitrary governance, and though they sent rice to Edo, not only was none sent to the Emperor's residence of Kyoto, but people who tried to buy amounts of rice as small as five to ten *shō* (9–18 liters) were apprehended. This is exactly like the [Chinese] lord, Ge Bo, who killed farming children for carrying lunches—unspeakable! In every land, the people are under the rule of the Tokugawa House without distinction, so the carrying out of such discriminatory acts is the result of a complete lack of benevolence by the commissioners and their subordinates. Moreover, they constantly circulated self-serving official orders, and, as detailed earlier, they treated only the parasitic Osaka people with consideration. It is because they are personages of low character, lacking basic moral virtues, totally lacking any human sensitivity.

Among the three great cities, it is the wealthy of Osaka who for years have made loans to all the daimyo, commanding usurious interest and manipulating vast purchases of rice and accumulating unprecedented wealth. They live as if they were the senior retainers of daimyo despite their status as townspeople, and they dislocate all manner of farming lands for mansions, living lives without wants. Knowing of the recent disasters of Heaven, they do not tremble with fear. Although people die of starvation and beg in the streets they refuse to aid them, instead dining on delicacies and feasting extravagantly, they keep mistresses in special residences, invite daimyo and their retainers to houses of pleasure, and drink expensive saké as if it were water. In this season of disasters they wear silk, hire jesters and dancing girls as if they were enjoying the pleasures of ordinary times, as if they were King Zhou in his all night feasts. Just like King Zhou, by inviting the commissioners and other officials to such entertainment, these people hold power in the palms of their hands, and it is impossible to save the common people. Day in and day out, they manipulate the rice markets, making themselves veritable salary-robbers. It is exceedingly difficult to realize the essence of the Heavenly Way of the Ancient Sages, and no attempt is being made to attain it.

At this juncture, those of us who have watched from seclusion—although we have neither the power of Tang nor the virtue of Confucius and Mencius—knowing that it is for the benefit of the world which has been left without champions, we bring disaster upon our families, unite with those of high purpose, and punish these officials and the luxuriating wealthy townspeople of Osaka. We will attack and kill them, taking the wealth that they have hidden away in holes and storerooms, taking the gold, silver, copper cash and grains that are hidden in warehouses and mete out all of these.

To the people of Settsu, Kawachi, Izumi, and Harima: Whether you have no fields or even if you do but without enough to support your husbands, wives, children, and ancestors, if on any day you hear of an uprising in Osaka, depart immediately regardless of the distance and come running to Osaka where we will distribute money and rice. The warehouses will be opened to the commoners as were the fabulous storehouses by the last will of King Wu, saving the people from the present famine and misfortune. If moreover there are men with the equipment and abilities, they should all join together to form a military force to punish crooked men. This is most certainly not a plan for peasant uprisings or the like. We will reduce each and every one of the taxes and duties. We will restore everything to the political way of the Jimmu Emperor, and effect a management of things with great magnanimity and bounteousness. Thereby we will also wash away completely the extravagant and corrupt habits which have multiplied with the years.

We will return to humble simplicity; with gratitude to the Heavenly blessings of the Four Seas, we will nourish fathers, mothers, wives and children. Rescuing them from a living hell, we will bring before their very eyes a living paradise. Though it would be difficult to return to the age of Yao and Shun or Amaterasu, we will restore the essential quality of the flourishing days of Jimmu. We want this document spread to each and every village, but as there are so many, let it be posted on shrines and temples of the large villages where many houses are gathered, and let it be spread quickly so that it may be communicated to all villages around Osaka, and yet so that their watchmen do not learn of it. If by chance it is discovered by any of the watchmen and they appear to intend to report it to the wicked scoundrels of the four places outside Osaka where outcasts congregate, unite without hesitation and strike them all down without exception.

To those who learn of the occurrence of a great uprising and, out of doubt, do not come running, or come late and the riches of the wealthy have all been burned to ashes such that the bounty of the country has been lost—do not in any way bear a grudge against us afterwards and whisper that we are bandits who destroy such stores; for we have given notice to all in order to prevent this. Moreover, shred and burn all documents that the headmen and other village officials have gathered for taxation. This can only be thought of as an act of deep consideration, which has the intent of saving the people from great suffering.

Some may compare this event to the rebellions of our country's Taira no Masakado [a tenth-century pretender to the throne] or Akechi Mitsuhide [assassin of the great unifier Oda Nobunaga] and the Han dynasty's Liu Yu [warlord accused of plotting to seize the throne] or Zhu Yuan Zhang [peasant founder of Ming dynasty]. Although there may be a connection, our actions do not arise in the least from a desire to seize the country, but from the Heavenly mirror of the sun, moon, stars, and comets. In the final analysis, Tang and Wu, and the Han and Ming founders mourned for the people and acted only from sincere hearts to carry out the punishment of Heaven. If this seems suspicious to you, then simply open your eyes and observe closely how we end our enterprise.

Priests and physicians, read this document with care to the commoners. If you shrink from the danger of being caught by the headmen or elders and hide yourself from them, then you will be sought out for punishment.

Sacrificing to Heaven, we enact Heaven's punishment.

3

Ordinances Issued by the Shogunate
1841–1842

The death of the long-reigning eleventh shogun, Ienari, freed shogunal officials to embark on reforms to deal with Japan's internal and external problems. The Opium War (1839–1842), which ended in China's defeat at the hands of the British, suggested to them that the 1825 directive to drive foreign ships away had been a mistake. Instead, foreigners were to be given the supplies they needed and then sent on their way. To bring down prices, seen as a primary cause of the previous years' unrest, officials abolished the guilds that regulated trade between Osaka and Edo. They also tried to rationalize the landholding system in the regions around Osaka and Edo by confiscating land held by the shogun's direct retainers and vassal daimyo and replacing it with land farther away.

Most of the directives centered on what officials saw as pernicious customs that wasted money and encouraged moral laxity. They discouraged the daimyo from giving the shogun expensive presents and tried to reassert the shogun's authority over the daimyo by reminding them of their long-standing obligations. The majority of the ordinances concerned commoners, who in the officials' eyes were enjoying themselves entirely too much. By examining the ordinances telling commoners what not to do, historians can glimpse the changes wrought by a commercial revolution in town and country.

October 15, 1841: Official Pronouncement

It is rumored that many daimyo postpone their regularly scheduled visits to serve the shogun [in Edo] using illness as an excuse, or [not wanting to return to their domains] receive leave from the shogun to return home but remain in the capital claiming to be ill. In recent years an especially large number have petitioned to stay in the capital, and some have not gone home for years. While illness is something that

Suzuki Tōzo and Koike Shōtarō, eds., *Fujiokaya nikki*, vol. 2 (Tokyo: San'ichi Shobō, 1988), 214–15, 222–23, 225, 238, 239, 247, 248, 266–68, 276, 289, 290, 298. Translated by Anne Walthall.

cannot be helped, once you are well enough you should resolve to serve at the regularly appointed time or else not loiter in the capital. If you are strong enough to make the journey with effort, you will be encouraged to go home.

December 7, 1841: Directive to the Commoner Wards

Hereafter expensive sweets and dishes that require too much useless preparation are unnecessary. Even though they have been made up to now, this is to stop.

Gold, silver, gold gilt, and gold foil are not to be used on bows for boys, decorative helmets and swords, or battledores [light rackets] used as New Year's decorations.

Dolls for girls over 8.5 inches in height are unnecessary. Anything shorter, that costs little money, and that is dressed in clothes for servants is okay.

Toy utensils are of course not to be decorated with embossed gold lacquer, and lacquer with gold dust should only be used for the family crest.

It is forbidden to trade in expensive potted plants.

It is unnecessary for women's clothing to have an elaborate pattern or embroidery.

All of the townspeople are to understand that they are not to shoot off fireworks. Henceforth neither men nor women are to use luxurious items unsuitable to their status, and indeed if there be anyone who uses elaborate items, even including hair ornaments, as soon as members of their group catch sight of this, they are to verify name and address, have ward officials accompany them, and take the offender immediately to the magistrate's office for an investigation.

There were notices to this effect in the Kyōhō and Kansei eras and afterward as well, but with the passage of years, everywhere the world has become flamboyant, no one considers his status but competes in fashion, and we have heard that even those who are inconspicuous on the outside actually trade in expensive goods for no reason at all.

December 18, 1841: Notice Sent in All Directions

We have heard that people in the countryside waste money by making costumes and utensils and amassing curiosities for entertainments labeled festivals to the gods, ceremonies for driving insects away from the crops, or prayers for good harvests that are just like plays and spectacles. This is outrageous. People who make arrangements for such things or who make their livelihood through them are absolutely not to enter the villages, and that goes as well for traveling merchants of bad character, outcasts, and so forth. As a matter of course, the neglect of cultivation comes from following examples of bad things such as pleasure seeking and laziness, and this leads to abandoned fields and the depths of poverty that finally lead to the village's dissolution. . . . From here on out, it is strictly forbidden to bring people together for amusements, Kabuki, story chanting, dancing, and all forms of plays.

December 1841: Notice Sent to the Edo Theaters

At this time the shogun intends to reform customs in the city. Recently actors have taken to living in the vicinity of the theaters where they mingle with the townspeople. In addition, the three theaters' productions infect urban customs because they have become extremely lewd. The plays have become particularly vulgar recently, and since what becomes the latest fad often arises from the theater, regardless of how things were before, having them positioned in the city close to the castle has become a matter of concern to the shogun. All actors belong to a discriminated against status, and since it is a matter of poor administration for the gap [between them and ordinary commoners] to have somehow disappeared, at this time the two theaters in the Sakai and Ashiya wards, as well as the puppet theater and the townspeople's houses connected to them, are ordered to move away. Since there will probably be various hardships associated with leaving land where they have resided for two hundred years, they will receive suitable recompense.

January 1842: Directive to the Wards

For a long time, no one called herself a hairdresser for women, no one tied up women's hair, no one made this her business, nor did any women pay money to have their hair fixed. Recently, however, places that specialize in dressing women's hair have appeared, and they model their designs on courtesans and the Kabuki actors who take female roles (*onnagata*). As a consequence clothing and other items become beautifully ornamented, this disrupts customs, and so forth. What can the parents and husbands of women who have their hair dressed be thinking? Women too should keep it in mind to maintain a suitable appearance. Henceforth the wives and daughters of the lower classes should remember to dress their own hair and not to have it dressed by a hairdresser for women. The women who have dressed women's hair up to now are to change their household's occupation to manual work suitable for women such as sewing or laundry.

April 9, 1842: Directive Issued by Senior Councilor Mizuno Tadakuni

Although practice halls for martial arts are supposed to be supervised, we have heard that in recent years people who misbehave have appeared, few practice seriously with diligence, and some just engage in idle talk and so forth.

In recent years people declare that they have a license for the martial arts, but some have spent few years in training, and others are immature youths. Becoming skilled depends on the quickness and versatility of one's temperament and also on the circumstances of one's practice. Although skill must not be attributed wholly to the number of years [spent in training], it is a mistake to want to get a license as soon as possible or to want to compete when one is still inexperienced. It is also not a good thing for teachers to feel compelled to transmit their secrets just because it has become the fashion.

April 18, 1842: Directive to the Wards

We have heard that among people with no fixed occupation, some advocate tattooing, carve all sorts of pictures or writing all over their bodies, outline them in black ink, and add colors. This sort of thing has an impact on customs. Although anyone ought to be ashamed to wound an otherwise healthy body, is it because young people take it to be flashy? They do not understand that everyone secretly ridicules them. Because it is not good to wear tattoos, henceforth no one is to tattoo his or her entire body, not even on the hands and feet.

Now as for the people who do the tattooing, although they claim that they simply give people what they want, they are not to draw anything abhorrent. To carve tattoos in accordance with people's preferences is inexcusable.

We have heard that for people who make their living as firefighters or palanquin bearers, not to have a tattoo means that they cannot join the guild.

April 25, 1842: Directive to the Wards

In the town women are teaching songs, chants, and samisen [stringed musical instrument] to warriors and townspeople alike, and this has given rise to rumors of lewdness. Men should teach men. Female instructors should not have male pupils, particularly those who wear swords. Even in the case of townspeople, there have been directives in the past that practices taught by women to men are unnecessary.

May 5, 1842: Government Directive

We have heard that recently people have been gambling in the daimyo compounds. Because orders to strictly obey the intent of directives issued in the Kansei era have recently arrived, it goes without saying that there should be strict orders to everyone, including servants, to stop. You are to understand that the city magistrate and the units that investigate robberies and fires have been instructed to make patrols and raid the compounds to make arrests.

May 20, 1842: Government Directive

There have been repeated directives not to secretly trade in vegetables out of season. Recently demand for the first goods of the year has expanded, and restaurants and tea shops compete to purchase them. It is outrageous that they prepare such expensive items. Since this luxury comes from people raising things such as cucumbers, eggplants, various kinds of green beans, and sprouts by hanging shutters to keep out the rain or else heating a room with balls of charcoal to grow vegetables out of season all year round, the sellers too are absolutely outrageous.

Fish and birds are to be sold once they have been caught in the wild, and it is strictly forbidden to waste manpower and great expense to figure out a way to raise them in order to sell them for a high price.

June 12, 1842: Directive Issued by Senior Councilor Mizuno Tadakuni

Neither samurai with the right of audience [with the shogun], those without, nor those with merely the status to wear *hakama* [pleated trousers, i.e., samurai] are to allow the men or children in their hereditary retainers' families who will not inherit the family name and occupation to be adopted by their hired servants. Although a directive to this effect was issued in 1793, we have heard that in recent years some people have acted improperly. Since those who are hired servants are restricted by their status to being servants, for someone of a different status to become an adopted son causes the cherished status of hereditary retainer to be forgotten for the sake of mere convenience.

July 11, 1842: Directive to the Wards

Henceforth books are to focus on loyalty, filial piety, chastity, and restraint, which will improve children and women.

Once new editions are ready, they are to be presented to the city magistrate for inspection.

Pictures that continue for more than three pages and erotic books of all sorts are not to be sold at all.

October 21, 1842: Injunctions to Farmers

From ancient times it has been the custom for farmers to wear rough clothing and tie their hair with straw, but recently with the spread of luxury, they have been wearing items unsuitable to their status. Not only are they putting oil on their hair and using hair ties, but also although they should be wearing straw raincoats and hats as rain gear, now following the example of popular fads, they carry umbrellas and wear oilskin raincoats. Everything else goes along with this, causing lots of useless expenses, and it is deplorable that the fields and rice paddies handed down from the farmers' ancestors end up with strangers. It is only recently that those who make a sideline of selling saké and food have appeared among the farmers, and we find bathhouses and hairdressers. As a matter of course [these practices] lead young people astray. Because they are the basis for weakness and debauchery, it is essential that people return to the customs of the past, practice simplicity in all things, and encourage agriculture. Since we abolished the wholesalers who monopolized ship transport as well as other guilds, we have heard that now inside the capital there are a number of shops conducting similar enterprises. As a matter of course they may have pushed out into rural areas, but it is a mistake to see the wards in the capital and the countryside as being the same. The farmers' status requires them to use their strength chiefly for cultivation. They are not to shift to sidelines and begin the businesses pursued by townspeople.

We have heard that in recent years many farm men and women seek employment; as a matter of course wages go up, and in particular the women called weaving girls collect entirely too much in wages. This all happens because they run after sideline work, which confuses the proper order of things. Unlike the townspeople, farmers have to pay particular attention to managing their enterprises with enough profit for the moment. They should carefully understand this, devote themselves wholeheartedly to agriculture, and resolve not to lose their fields and paddies.

Disownment, breaking off relations, and taking people off the family register are all serious matters. Only a person who was poorly educated would be able to go so far as to sever familial bonds. It goes without saying that people who have a son or burdensome relative must take this to heart and so must all of the village officials. It is essential that they manage things so that the population does not decline by even a single person.

November 3, 1842: Warning

Recently cargo ships that take the northern route, but also ships from other provinces, have been setting sails that resemble those of foreign ships. They have already been mistaken for foreign ships, even though our ships are not to carry three sails. There are reports that in contrast to the past, they appear to be going out into the Pacific, and we have heard that some are sailing close to the coast of Korea.

December 31, 1842: Directive

We do not care if people who call themselves women's doctors in the city properly perform gynecological medical treatments, but we have heard that some of them may perform abortions at the request of women who are pregnant. This is unforgiveable.

2

The Coming of the West

4

MILLARD FILLMORE

Letter to the Emperor of Japan
November 13, 1852

In 1851 U.S. president Millard Fillmore announced that a naval expedition would be sent to Japan to secure "friendship, commerce, a supply of coal and provisions, and protection for our shipwrecked people." He appointed Commodore Matthew C. Perry (1794–1858), who had seen action in several wars, to command the expedition. Instead of trying to deal with Japanese officials at Nagasaki, where Dutch and Chinese ships were permitted to land, Perry headed directly for Edo Bay. He arrived at Uraga on July 8, 1853, and advancing with his four warships as far as Kanagawa (close to present-day Yokohama), he insisted on delivering a letter from President Fillmore to the emperor of Japan, though the letter ended up with the shogunate instead. Perry then withdrew to Hong Kong, promising to return (with additional warships) in the spring of 1854 for an answer to the American request for treaty relations.

Fillmore's letter, coupled with a similar request from a Russian envoy in Nagasaki, initiated a period of intense political, economic, and social unrest. On the one hand, foreign demands to "open the country" encouraged a nationalism akin to xenophobia; on the other hand, they made some degree of westernization inevitable. Without Western guns and ships, Japan could not protect itself against the foreign threat. In the end,

Francis L. Hawks, *Narrative of the Expedition of an American Squadron to the China Seas and Japan, Performed in the Years 1852, 1853, and 1854, under the Command of Commodore M. C. Perry, United States Navy, by Order of the Government of the United States* (Washington, D.C.: Congress of the United States, 1856), 256–57.

Perry and his "black ships" began a process that, along with intractable domestic problems, destroyed the Tokugawa regime economically, militarily, and politically.

MILLARD FILLMORE, President of the United States of America to his Imperial Majesty, THE EMPEROR OF JAPAN

Great and Good Friend: I send you this public letter by Commodore Matthew C. Perry, an officer of the highest rank in the navy of the United States, and commander of the squadron now visiting your imperial majesty's dominions.

I have directed Commodore Perry to assure your imperial majesty that I entertain the kindest feelings toward your majesty's person and government, and that I have no other object in sending him to Japan but to propose to your imperial majesty that the United States and Japan should live in friendship and have commercial intercourse with each other.

The Constitution and laws of the United States forbid all interference with the religious or political concerns of other nations. I have particularly charged Commodore Perry to abstain from every act which could possibly disturb the tranquility of your imperial majesty's dominions.

The United States of America reach from ocean to ocean, and our Territory of Oregon and State of California lie directly opposite to the dominions of your imperial majesty. Our steamships can go from California to Japan in eighteen days.

Our great State of California produces about sixty millions of dollars in gold every year, besides silver, quicksilver, precious stones, and many other valuable articles. Japan is also a rich and fertile country, and produces many very valuable articles. Your imperial majesty's subjects are skilled in many of the arts. I am desirous that our two countries should trade with each other, for the benefit both of Japan and the United States.

We know that the ancient laws of your imperial majesty's government do not allow of foreign trade, except with the Chinese and the Dutch; but as the state of the world changes and new governments are formed, it seems to be wise, from time to time, to make new laws. There was a time when the ancient laws of your imperial majesty's government were first made.

About the same time America, which is sometimes called the New World, was first discovered and settled by the Europeans. For a long time there were but a few people, and they were poor. They have now become quite numerous; their commerce is very extensive; and they think that if your imperial majesty were so far to change the ancient laws as to allow a free trade between the two countries it would be extremely beneficial to both.

If your imperial majesty is not satisfied that it would be safe altogether to abrogate the ancient laws which forbid foreign trade, they might be suspended for five or ten years, so as to try the experiment. If it does not prove as beneficial as was hoped, the ancient laws can be restored. The United States often limit their treaties with foreign States to a few years, and then renew them or not, as they please.

I have directed Commodore Perry to mention another thing to your imperial majesty. Many of our ships pass every year from California to China; and great numbers of our people pursue the whale fishery near the shores of Japan. It sometimes happens, in stormy weather, that one of our ships is wrecked on your imperial majesty's shores. In all such cases we ask, and expect, that our unfortunate people should be treated with kindness, and that their property should be protected, till we can send a vessel and bring them away. We are very much in earnest in this.

Commodore Perry is also directed by me to represent to your imperial majesty that we understand there is a great abundance of coal and provisions in the Empire of Japan. Our steamships, in crossing the great ocean, burn a great deal of coal, and it is not convenient to bring it all the way from America. We wish that our steamships and other vessels should be allowed to stop in Japan and supply themselves with coal, provisions, and water. They will pay for them in money, or anything else your imperial majesty's subjects may prefer; and we request your imperial majesty to appoint a convenient port, in the southern part of the Empire, where our vessels may stop for this purpose. We are very desirous of this.

These are the only objects for which I have sent Commodore Perry, with a powerful squadron, to pay a visit to your imperial majesty's renowned city of Yedo: friendship, commerce, a supply of coal and provisions, and protection for our shipwrecked people.

We have directed Commodore Perry to beg your imperial majesty's acceptance of a few presents. They are of no great value in themselves; but some of them may serve as specimens of the articles manufactured in the United States, and they are intended as tokens of our sincere and respectful friendship.

May the Almighty have your imperial majesty in His great and holy keeping!

In witness whereof, I have caused the great seal of the United States to be hereunto affixed, and have subscribed the same with my name, at the city of Washington, in America, the seat of my government, on the thirteenth day of the month of November, in the year one thousand eight hundred and fifty-two.

[Seal attached]

Your good friend,
MILLARD FILLMORE, President

5

Debate on Opening the Country
August 1853

Commodore Perry and his black ships placed the shogunate in a quandary. The chief senior councilor, Abe Masahiro, took an extraordinary measure in responding to the crisis. Rather than continue to restrict policy deliberations to his peers, he asked Tokugawa officials, the daimyo, and a few Tokugawa retainers, scholars, and merchants for their opinions. Some wanted to open the country to the West; others maintained that the foreign barbarians must be expelled no matter what the cost. Aware of the power of American cannon, most sought to avoid war.

The exchange between Tokugawa Nariaki, retired head of the Mito domain and proponent of expulsion, and Abe Masahiro makes clear the impossible dilemma confronting the shogunate: Both choices, war or peace, could lead to national collapse. Nariaki wanted to confront the foreign threat by ordering the daimyo to prepare for war. His strategy was designed to stimulate the sort of nationalism that would cause people, regardless of status or domain affiliation, to rise in defense of their country. Abe Masahiro advocated a more "realistic" policy of compromise with Perry's demands. It was too early, he argued, to engage the enemy.

Baba Bun'ei, *Japan, 1853–1864; or, Genji Yume Monogatari*, trans. Ernest Mason Satow (Tokyo: Naigai Shuppan Kyōkai, 1905), 5–8. Translation modified by the editors.

Tokugawa Nariaki: The Barbarians have been watching our country with greedy eyes for many years, and the question is therefore nothing new. Still our Empire has its laws which have descended from our ancestors, and those laws declare that when any barbarian ship approaches our shores, it is to be driven off by force, without a second thought; and they were so afraid that they did not venture to bring their vessels into our inner seas except at Nagasaki. But some years ago [1842], Mizuno Tadakuni, who was then chief senior councilor, issued a benevolent order, by which the driving out of barbarian ships was prohibited. Ever since then, the barbarians have kept a greedy eye on our country. If we are frightened now by their aggressive lying stratagems and give them what they ask for (as their designs are both cunning and treacherous), they will go on from bad to worse.

At first they will give us philosophical instruments, machinery and other curiosities. They will take advantage of ignorant people, and trade being their chief object, will manage bit by bit to impoverish the country; after which they will treat us just as they like; perhaps behave with the greatest rudeness and insult us, and end by swallowing up Japan. If we don't drive them away now we shall never have another opportunity. If now we resort to a willfully dilatory method of proceeding, we shall deeply regret it later when it will be of no use.

Abe Masahiro: If we try to drive the foreigners away, they will immediately commence hostilities, and then we shall be obliged to fight. If we once get into a dispute we shall have an enemy to fight who will not be easily disposed of. He does not care how long a time he will have to spend over it, but he will come with several myriads of men of war and surround our shores completely: he will capture our junks and blockade our ports and deprive us of all hope of protecting our coasts. However large a number of his ships we might destroy, he is so accustomed to that sort of thing, that he would not care in the least. Even supposing that our troops were animated by patriotic zeal in the commencement of the war, after they had been fighting for several years their patriotic zeal would naturally wane; the soldiers would become fatigued, and we should have ourselves to thank for this. Soldiers who have distinguished themselves are rewarded by grants of land, or else you attack and seize the enemy's territory and that becomes your own property; so every man is encouraged to fight his best. But in a war with foreign countries, a man may undergo hardship for years, may fight as if his life were worth nothing, and as all the land in this country has already owners, there will be none to be given away as rewards; so we should have to give rewards in words or money. In time Japan would be put to an immense expense and the people be plunged into misery. Rather than allow this, as we are not the equals of foreigners in the mechanical arts, let us have intercourse with foreign countries, learn their drill and tactics, and when we have made the nation as united as one family, we shall be able to go abroad and give lands in foreign countries to those who have distinguished themselves in battle; the soldiers will vie with one another to display their courage, and it will not be too late then to declare war. Now we shall have to defend ourselves against these foreign enemies skilled in the use of mechanical appliances, with our soldiers whose military skill has considerably diminished during a long peace of three hundred years, and we certainly could not feel sure of victory, especially in a naval war.

6

The President of the Foreign Temple of the United Mountains of America

1854

How did commoners react to the arrival of Commodore Perry and his black ships? With a mixture of fear and curiosity. Crude broadsheets, the forerunners of newspapers, often focused on the unusual and grotesque, along with other news items interesting enough to turn a profit. The arrival of foreigners in Edo Bay was one such occasion. In 1853 and 1854, more than five hundred broadsheets appeared for sale in the streets of Edo. They described the black ships, examined the government's attempt at coastal defense, tried to satisfy the curiosity of the townspeople with information about America and world geography, and poked fun at Tokugawa helplessness.

Some of the broadsheets, such as the one included here, were antiforeign in character and reveal the existence of a sort of commoner nationalism. It used Buddhist terminology to help people understand the significance of Perry's visit. The "president" in the title refers to President

Yokohama Archives of History, Yokohama, Kanagawa Prefecture. Translated by M. William Steele.

Millard Fillmore (Document 4). According to the title, he is from a foreign temple called "America." Its "mountain name," a common secondary title for temples, is "United Mountains," a pun on the United States.

The black ships set many patriots and "men of high purpose" on a path that would lead to the Meiji Restoration. The story of the different ways in which they responded—from a determination to learn from the West to xenophobic nationalism—and their loss of faith in Tokugawa authority is well-known. Broadsheets provide good evidence that commoners responded in similarly diverse ways.

Courtesy of the Yokohama Archives of History.

Image of the President of the Foreign Temple of the United Mountains of America

This image is the same as that of the Coal Avatar of the Mountains. The slippery-tongued monk Perry in his berserk state has come in a steamship from 5,000 *ri* [about 12,000 miles] away, bringing with him the barbarian Adams as his acolyte, who helps him reveal the image of the president to the countries of the world. In fact, Perry is making a fool of the countries of the world by using the image of the president for his own ends and chanting a sutra that repeatedly begs for trade. He has revealed this image to China, India, and Holland. Now he has come begging to our exalted country. The image that he brings with him will startle everyone. It will cost the warriors much money; it will ruin the businesses of the merchants; it will cause the peasants great suffering. On its head it wears an arrogant crown; in its right hand it carries a gun and bayonet; from its left hand hangs a depth-sounding rope; from its mouth pours great praise of its own country, but its chest is so full of evil spirits that it has a smokestack coming out of its back to expel fire and smoke. Because of this, its ships are often in distress with no time to let down anchor. Since it knows no safety at sea, it drifts with the waves and its food supplies become exhausted. The image lands here and there on islands, where it reveals its true nature as the wild and fearsome sword-wielding Vidyaraja Myôô [a wrathful Buddhist deity]. Its esoteric words are: "I have given you the letter twice; hurry up and reply or else." The gang of capricious officers is far away, so come and see the black ships.

7

Townsend Harris's Advice to the Shogunate
1857

Commodore Perry concluded Japan's first foreign treaty, the Treaty of Peace and Amity between the United States of America and Japan, also known as the Treaty of Kanagawa, in 1854. Tokugawa negotiators managed to reject demands for commercial relations, but they agreed to open two ports, Shimoda and Hakodate, to American ships and promised aid to whalers in distress. Their greatest concession was to allow an American consul to take up residence in Shimoda.

Townsend Harris (1804–1878) arrived in Shimoda in 1856. He sought immediately to negotiate a more conventional trade treaty

From *Papers Relating to the Foreign Relations of the United States, 1878*, 620–36, Government Printing Office, 1879, as it appears in M. William Steele, "Townsend Harris on the Art of Diplomacy: Some Documents in Translation," *Asian Cultural Studies* 35 (2009): 210, 212–14.

*and open formal diplomatic relations. As he wrote in his journal on
August 19, 1856, "I shall be the first recognized agent from a civilized
power to reside in Japan. This forms an epoch in my life and may be the
beginning of a new order of things in Japan."[1] The "new order" did not
come easily. Harris repeatedly requested permission to travel to Edo to
initiate negotiations on trade and permanent residence for American
merchants, but it took a year for Japanese officials to grant his request.
Harris entered Edo on November 30, 1857, and after intricate preparations had been made for the unprecedented audience, he delivered
his credentials to Tokugawa Iesada, the thirteenth shogun. Afterward,
Harris met with the shogun's chief senior councilor, Hotta Masayoshi, to
enlighten him and other Tokugawa officials on the state of the world, the
development of modern industry, the threat of British imperialism, and
the benefits to be derived by concluding a treaty with the United States.*

Statement Made by the American Ambassador in the House of Hotta Masayoshi

It is the uniform custom of the United States, while frequently making treaties with other countries, not to annex any country merely by
force of arms. Many changes have taken place in the West within the
last fifty years. Since the invention of steamships distant countries have
become like those that are near at hand. Since the invention of the elec-
tric telegraphy especially, rapid communications may be had between
the most distant parts. By means of this instrument a reply may be had
in an hour to a message sent from Edo to Washington. By means of
steam one can go from California to Japan in eighteen days. Commerce
has become very extensive since the invention of steam, and the countries of the West have in consequence become rich. The nations of the
West hope that by means of steam communication all of the world will
become as one family. Any nation that refuses to hold intercourse with
other nations must expect to be excluded from this family. No nation has
the right to refuse to hold intercourse with others.

. . . Opium is the one great enemy of China. If it is used it weakens
the body and injures it like the most deadly poison; it makes the rich
poor and the wise foolish; it unmans all that use it, and by reason of the

---

[1]Townsend Harris, *The Complete Journal of Townsend Harris: First American Consul
General and Minister to Japan*, introduction and notes by Mario Emilio Consenza (New
York: Doubleday, Doran, 1930), 196.

misery it brings, robbery and acts of violence increase. About one thousand criminals are executed annually for crimes committed while under the influence of opium; but notwithstanding this punishment, crimes are on the increase. The uncle of the reigning Emperor of China died from the effects of opium. The opium used in China comes from India, which is subject to England.

Though "opium" is, as I have already said, a very bad thing for China, England will not prohibit it, because the trade is profitable. Hence the word "opium" is not used in the treaty between the two countries.

. . . It appears that the English think that the Japanese, too, are fond of opium, and they want to bring it here also. If a man use opium once he cannot stop it, and it becomes a life-long habit to use opium; hence the English want to introduce it into Japan. . . .

The President [of the United States] wishes the Japanese to be very prudent about the introduction of opium, and if a treaty is made, he wishes that opium may be strictly prohibited. . . .

The President assures you that if you have intercourse with other countries, and allow agents to reside in the capital, the country will be quite safe. I must congratulate your country that no war has taken place for hundreds of years; but peace, when continued too long, may be injurious, as thereby the military power may become weak and inefficient.

The President regards the Japanese as a brave people; but courage, though useful in time of war, is subordinate to knowledge of arts; hence, courage without such knowledge is not to be highly esteemed. In time of war steamships and improved arms are the most important things. If war should break out between England and Japan, the latter would suffer much more than the former. . . .

The President wants to make a treaty that will be honorable to Japan, without war, in a peaceable manner, after deliberate consultation. If Japan should make a treaty with the ambassador of the United States, who has come unattended by military force, her honor will not be impaired. There will be a great difference between a treaty made with a single individual, unattended, and one made with a person who should bring fifty men-of-war to these shores. We were sent to this country by the President, who desires to promote the welfare of Japan, and are quite different from the ambassadors of other countries. We do not wish you to open your ports to foreign trade all at once. It will be quite satisfactory if you open them gradually, as the circumstances may require; but the President assures you that this will not be the case if you make a treaty with England first.

If you make a treaty first with the United States and settle the matter of the opium trade, England cannot change this, though she should desire to do so. . . .

It is the usual custom of these days to transport the superabundant productions of one country to where they are wanted, so that there may be an equalization. If, for instance, there should be a scarcity of food in England, those countries where food is abundant will send the needed supplies, even if they have to interrupt the usual trade. I do not mean by the word "trade" only the exchange of marketable articles, but also the exchange of profitable new inventions. By trade the people of any one nation will become well acquainted with the productions and customs of all other countries. . . .

. . . America will furnish to Japan men-of-war, steamers, and needed arms, also officers of the army and navy, as many as may be required.

The President wishes it to be understood that should difficulty arise between Japan and any foreign country, he will gladly become a mediator, and use his good offices in the interest of peace.

8

Treaty of Amity and Commerce
July 29, 1858

Negotiated between Townsend Harris, consul general of the United States, and the foreign magistrates Inoue Kiyonao and Iwase Tadanari, the treaty signed on July 29, 1858, opened Japan to trade with the United States and provided new opportunities for social and cultural contact with the West. The only areas previously open to foreign contact were Shimoda and Hakodate, which had been opened in accordance with the 1854 Treaty of Kanagawa, also known as the Treaty of Peace and Amity. Under this treaty, five ports, including Kanagawa (later specified as Yokohama), were opened to trade, though some of these ports were far removed from major cities (Map 3). Religious freedom was allowed only

Hunter Miller, ed., *Treaties and Other International Acts of the United States of America*, vol. 7, *Documents 173–200, 1855–1858* (Washington, D.C.: Government Printing Office, 1942), 947–61.

in these ports, and trade in opium was prohibited. This treaty served as a prototype for treaties with other Western countries (a treaty with Holland was signed on August 18, with Russia on August 19, with Great Britain on August 26, and with France in October). The treaty was written in English, Japanese, and Dutch; the Dutch version is considered to be the original.

These treaties allowed Japan to escape some of the harsher conditions of the "unequal treaty" system imposed on China. Japan was deprived of tariff autonomy and forced to agree to extraterritoriality (whereby Westerners were declared outside the jurisdiction of Japanese law), but broad areas of reciprocity were mandated. Diplomatic agents, for example, were to be stationed in Edo and Washington, D.C. Moreover, having the document signed by the shogun signaled Japan's resolve to be accepted as an equal within the Western diplomatic order of international laws and treaties. Japanese silk and tea merchants were eager to engage in international trade. Yokohama grew rapidly in the 1860s, becoming one of the largest treaty ports in Asia and the site of dynamic interaction between East and West.

The President of the United States of America and His Majesty the Ty-coon [shogun] of Japan, desiring to establish on firm and lasting foundations, the relations of peace and friendship now happily existing between the two countries, and to secure the best interests of their respective Citizens and Subjects, by encouraging, facilitating and regulating their industry and trade, have resolved to conclude a Treaty of Amity and Commerce, for this purpose. . . .

Article First

There shall henceforward be perpetual peace and friendship between the United States of America, and His Majesty the Ty-coon of Japan, and His Successors.

The President of the United States may appoint a Diplomatic Agent to reside in the City of Edo, and Consuls or Consular Agents, to reside at any or all of the Ports in Japan, which are opened for American commerce, by this Treaty. The Diplomatic Agent and Consul General of the United States shall have the right to travel freely, in any part of the Empire of Japan, from the time they enter on the discharge of their official duties.

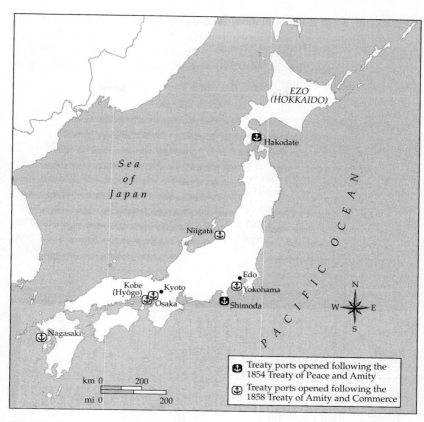

Map 3. *Treaty Ports in Japan, 1860s*

The Government of Japan may appoint a Diplomatic Agent, to reside in Washington, and Consuls or Consular Agents, for any or all of the Ports of the United States. The Diplomatic Agent and Consul General of Japan, may travel freely in any part of the United States, from the time they arrive in the Country.

Article Second

The President of the United States, at the request of the Japanese Government, will act as a friendly Mediator, in such matters of difference, as may arise between the Government of Japan, and any European Power.

The ships of war of the United States shall render friendly aid and assistance, to such Japanese vessels, as they may meet on the high seas, so far as can be done, without a breach of neutrality, and all American Consuls, residing at Ports visited by Japanese vessels shall also give them, such friendly aid.

Article Third

In addition to the Ports of Shimoda and Hakodate, the following Ports and Towns, shall be opened on the dates respectively appended to them.

Kanagawa [Yokohama], July 4, 1859

Nagasaki, July 4, 1859

Niigata, January 1, 1860

Hyōgo, January 1, 1863

Six months after the opening of Kanagawa, the Port of Shimoda shall be closed as a place of residence and trade, for American Citizens.

In all the foregoing Ports and Towns, American Citizens may permanently reside, they shall have the right to lease ground and purchase the buildings thereon, and may erect dwelling and warehouses. But no fortification or place of military strength, shall be erected under pretense of building dwelling or warehouses, and to see that this Article is observed, the Japanese Authorities shall have the right, to inspect from time to time any buildings, which are being erected, altered or repaired.

No wall, fence, or gate shall be erected by the Japanese, around the place of residence of the Americans, or anything done which may prevent a free egress and ingress to the same.

From January 1, 1862, Americans shall be allowed to reside in the City of Edo, and from January 1, 1863, in the City of Osaka, for the purposes of trade only. In each of these two Cities, a suitable place, within which they may hire houses, and the distance they may go, shall be arranged by the American Diplomatic Agent, and the Government of Japan.

Americans may freely buy from Japanese and sell to them, any articles that either may have for sale, without the intervention of any Japanese Officers, in such purchase or sale or in making or receiving payment for the same, and all classes of Japanese, may purchase, sell, keep or use any Articles sold to them, by the Americans.

Munitions of war shall only be sold to the Japanese Government and Foreigners.

No rice or wheat shall be exported from Japan, as cargo, but all Americans resident in Japan, and ships for their crews and passengers, shall be furnished with sufficient supplies of the same.

Americans, residing in Japan, shall have the right to employ Japanese as servants, or in any other capacity.

Article Fourth

Duties shall be paid, to the Government of Japan, on all goods landed in the Country, and on all Articles of Japanese production, that are exported as cargo, according to the Tariff hereunto appended.

The importation of opium is prohibited, and any American vessel coming to Japan, for the purposes of trade, having more than three catties (four pounds avoirdupois) weight of opium on board, such surplus quantity shall be seized, and destroyed by the Japanese Authorities.

Article Fifth

All foreign coin shall be current in Japan, and pass for its corresponding weight of Japanese coin, of the same description.

Article Sixth

Americans, committing offences against Japanese, shall be tried in American Consular Courts, and when guilty, shall be punished according to American Law.

Japanese, committing offences against Americans, shall be tried by the Japanese Authorities, and punished according to Japanese Law.

The Consular Courts shall be open to Japanese Creditors, to enable them to recover their just claims, against American Citizens, and the

Japanese Courts shall in like manner be open to American Citizens, for the recovery of their just claims, against Japanese.

Article Seventh

In the open Harbors of Japan, Americans shall be free to go where they please, within the following limits.

At Kanagawa, the River Logo [Rokugo] (which empties into the Bay of Edo between Kawasaki and Shinagawa) and Ten Ri [about twenty-four miles] in any other direction.

At Hakodate, Ten Ri, in any direction.

At Hyōgo, Ten Ri, in any direction, that of Kyoto excepted, which City shall not be approached nearer than Ten Ri. The crews of vessels resorting to Hyōgo shall not cross the River Enagawa [Inagawa], which empties into the Bay between Hyōgo and Osaka. . . .

Americans, who have been convicted of felony, or twice convicted of misdemeanors, shall not go more than one Japanese Ri [about two and a half miles] inland from the places of their respective residences, and all Persons so convicted, shall lose their right of permanent residence in Japan, and the Japanese Authorities may require them to leave the Country.

Article Eighth

Americans in Japan, shall be allowed the free exercise of their Religion, and for this purpose shall have the right to erect suitable places of worship. No injury shall be done to such buildings, nor any insult be offered to the religious worship of the Americans.

American Citizens shall not injure any Japanese temple or shrine, or offer any insult or injury, to Japanese religious ceremonies, or to the objects of their worship.

The Americans and Japanese shall not do anything that may be calculated to excite religious animosity. The Government of Japan has already abolished the practice of trampling on religious emblems.

Article Ninth

When requested by the American Consul, the Japanese Authorities will cause the arrest of all deserters and fugitives from justice, receive in jail, all Persons, held as Prisoners by the Consul, and give to the Consul such assistance, as may be required to enable him, to enforce the observance of the Laws, by the Americans, who are on land, and to maintain order among the shipping.

Article Tenth

The Japanese Government may purchase or construct in the United States, ships of war, steamers, merchant ships, whale ships, cannon, munitions of war, and arms of all kinds, and any other things it may require. It shall have the right to engage in the United States, scientific, naval, and military men, artisans of all kinds, and mariners to enter into its service.

Article Thirteenth

After the 4th of July 1872, upon the desire of either the American or Japanese Governments, and on one year's notice given, by either party, this treaty and such portions of the Treaty of Kanagawa, as remain unrevoked by this Treaty, together with the regulations of trade, hereunto annexed, or those that may be hereafter introduced, shall be subject to revision by Commissioners, appointed on both sides, for this purpose, who will be empowered to decide on, and insert therein, such amendments, as experience shall prove to be desirable.

Treaty of Amity and Commerce, Between the United States of America and the Empire of Japan, Concluded at Yedo July 29, 1858; Ratification advised by Senate December 15, 1859; Ratified by President April 12, 1860; Ratifications Exchanged at Washington May 22, 1860; Proclaimed May 23, 1860.

3

Controversy and Purge

9

KUROSAWA TOKIKO

Appeal on Behalf of Tokugawa Nariaki
April 1859

*When it came time to sign the commercial treaty with Townsend Harris
(Document 8), the senior councilors decided that they needed the emper-
or's sanction. He refused to give it and urged the shogunate to appoint an
able man to be the next shogun. Newly appointed chief senior councilor
Ii Naosuke (1815–1860) signed the treaty anyway. Livid at this show of
disrespect, Tokugawa Nariaki, the lord of Mito, stormed into the castle
and berated him. Ii punished Nariaki for his unscheduled visit by forcing
him into strict house confinement, and when Mito retainers protested this
treatment of their loyal lord, he imprisoned them.*

*Among the commoners outraged at Ii's purge of imperial loyalists was
Kurosawa Tokiko (1806–1890), a schoolteacher and shaman. Determined to appeal Nariaki's unjust punishment to the imperial court, she
left Mito on March 26, 1859, arriving in Kyoto on April 27. There she
made a clear copy of her plea, written as a long poem, the traditional
medium for a lament. At the beginning she cited ancient poetry compila-
tions, and toward the end she alluded to the bow made from the catalpa
tree that was strummed by shamans to dispel evil.*

Shiryō 193 Kurosawa Tokiko "Kenjō no chōka" (Tenshi e hōken chōka). www.geocities
.jp/sybrma/193kurosawatokiko.chouka.html. Original text edited, annotated, and
published by Tatebayashi Miyatarō, *Bakumatsu ni okeru joryū kinnōka no taito: kinsei
ni okeru fujin kyōikuka no gensō, zōjū goi rikyō joshi to kenjō no chōka* (Ibaraki Pref.
Akatsuka: Tatebayashi Miyatarō, 1936). Translated by Anne Walthall.

When rumors spread that a secret female messenger had arrived in Kyoto, Tokiko fled to Osaka. There she was arrested and returned to Kyoto, where she underwent interrogation, a procedure later repeated in Edo. Deemed a political criminal, she spent months in prison before being sentenced to exile from Edo and her home in Mito.

In the ancient days of the myriad gods
The gods pacified Akitsushima [Japan];
Truly it is a noble country.
The pure light from the origin of the sun
Shines in the past, today, and tomorrow;
For a thousand years for all eternity to the tip of
Matsuyama is the changeless reign of our lord.
Our country's mistake of consenting to outrageous
Demands made over and over again by barbarians
Who know nothing of unchanging rule
Who come like white-capped waves
On their unstable foreign ships from other countries
Arose from the will of a warrior called Ii [Naosuke]
Even while eating a stipend bestowed
By our sacred country. How can he be considered
A man? He ordered the senseless, confused,
Black as a black current Manabe [Akikatsu]
To incarcerate our unparalleled, sagacious, and
Blameless lord [Tokugawa Nariaki]
Whose merits would be visible
Even in a swamp.
They scattered gold coins
Like the petals that fall from the wild mountain rose
Showing no awe of the lofty court above the clouds.
How despicable was their plot!
People of the floating world
Talked about such a shallow plot,
And by chance word of their evil deeds
Came to my hearing.
Though being low in status, because
I am descended from the illustrious Fujiwara, who
Come from the Sun Goddess's sacred descendants,
I could not ignore what I had heard.

Having reached the age of fifty-four,
To watch over my seventy-three-year-old
Mother's beautiful old age,
I took up the occupation of teacher and
Served her faithfully morning and night
By the thin smoke of the cooking fire,
Where we talked over the details
And I begged her for a short leave.
She agreed with me completely.
"Go quickly while you have the chance
For the sake of our country."
The words of this retired old woman
Immediately gave me strength.
At the dewy break of day as the sun rose
I left the province of Hitachi in traveling
Clothes, yearning for the imperial court
Where the ancient way of Japan prevails
And with my walking stick for support
Crossing under a traveler's sky,
Our sacred ruler's reign being my only thought.
Whether I went or returned across spring
Fields, the intrepid spirit in my old body
Pulled me like the spider's thread without
Slacking along the distant roads strung like
A catalpa bow, determined to cross the
Hanging bridge that goes above the clouds.
I am as dust born in the countryside far
From heaven and covered with dust, but
The wellspring in my heart as deep as a
Mountain well runs pure with gratitude for
Living in the realm of the Mito Tokugawa.
Without reflecting on my worthless self,
I racked my brains day and night over
What to do for the sake of the sacred country.
Determined on a single course of action,
I purified myself in the running water of
The Semi stream in my soiled traveling clothes
That I had worn for so long. At the first call of
The bush warbler offering best wishes for
The morning, perfume from the plum that
Flowers at the edge of the fields wafts its way

To heaven.
In awe and deference
I prostrate myself before the imperial court
Above the clouds and with the utmost
Reverence offer up my words.

Envoys
May the clear mirror that shines
Brightly for all eternity reflect
The pure heart of this base born person.

Having traveled distant roads strung
Like a catalpa bow, the spider's thread
Will pull me up above the clouds.

The heart of we Japanese is like
The moon just at dawn
That shines pure over Kiyomigata.

Wearing traveling clothes I left Hitachi [Mito]
Far behind to inquire about the reign
That follows the way of ancient Japan.

April 1859
Kurosawa Rikyō [sobriquet]
A second bow of reverence

10

YOSHIDA SHŌIN

Letter to Kitayama Yasuyo on the
Role of Dedicated Lower-Ranking People
May 9, 1859

Opposition to signing the commercial treaty against the emperor's wishes quickly spread beyond government circles to informed members of the samurai ruling class and the populace at large. Furious at this insult to His Majesty, Yoshida Shōin (1830–1859) called on "men of high purpose" and "grassroots heroes" to overthrow the Tokugawa regime and restore the emperor to power. For his advocacy of revolution, he was beheaded in prison like a common murderer, but he became a hero in modern Japan.

Born in Chōshū, a domain in southwestern Japan with a tradition of antipathy toward the Tokugawa regime, Shōin first studied Chinese military classics and later the works of Mencius that placed value on the people (as opposed to the ruling elite) and the need to confront arbitrary authority. He complemented his Confucian education with the study of the West, making several trips to Nagasaki to observe foreigners firsthand and pursuing Western military science. He also traveled to Mito to study with leaders of the Mito School of imperial loyalism, including Aizawa Seishisai (Document 1). Wishing to examine conditions in the West, he tried to board one of the American ships anchored at Shimoda in early 1854. He was arrested and returned to Chōshū, where, while technically confined to his house, he opened a school. His advocacy of imperial loyalism and his commitment to action inspired his students, many of whom played leading roles in the Meiji Restoration. He wrote the following letter while awaiting execution.

Meiji Japan through Contemporary Sources, vol. 2, *1844–1882* (Tokyo: Centre for East Asian Cultural Studies, 1970), 36–39. Translation modified.

I am writing from prison and, besides, what I have to say is based on conjecture, so it may very well strike you a bit odd.

Well, the general trend of the times has become fairly clear; the Divine Country's condition of imminent collapse is truly cause for great anxiety. The shogunate really is without men of talent. There may be some who can discuss adequately insignificant problems, but there is no one who can take a long-range view and set up a big plan. Especially the problem of dealing properly with the foreign barbarians—it is an extremely great problem now, one past a proper solution, and gradually, step by step, we find ourselves being controlled by the foreigners. Since 1853 and 1854, about six years have already passed and still there is no plan about making voyages [to foreign lands]. Where is Washington? What kind of a place is London? If we do not see the actual places, how can we deal with the matter?

Further, the officials of the shogunate are all of them meat-eating, uncivilized fellows and weaklings; even if there were among them one or two men of great stamp, as Mencius said, it will be impossible to curb the voices of a multitude of men. Hence, that the Eastern Tsin, the Southern Dynasties and the Song were unable to restore [Chinese rule to] the Central Plain [northern China] was only natural; how then is the present Tokugawa shogunate to do anything? As long as the Tokugawa [shogunate] continues to exist, it is impossible to imagine how far it will be controlled by America, Russia, England, and France. It makes one heave a sigh. Fortunately, at the very top we have a wise Emperor who is deeply concerned about this problem, but the court nobility is even more steeped in evil ways than the shogunate, and all they ever do is say that the Divine Country will be defiled if it lets the foreign barbarians approach, but they are unable to devise majestic plans as in days of yore. No wonder then that the [expel the barbarians] plan does not succeed. As for the lords of the various domains, all they do is curry favor with the shogunate, and they do not have any countermeasures at all. If the shogunate were to surrender to the foreign barbarians, they would have to follow suit and surrender also. Can any red-blooded person bear seeing Great Japan, which has for over three thousand years preserved its independence, at this late stage suffer the control of foreigners? Nothing less than a Napoleon back from the grave and chanting *"Vrijheid"* [freedom] can assuage the anguish in my breast.

I had no hopes of succeeding, of course, but since last year I have tried what little I can; my efforts availed me nothing, and I have ended up in prison. If I make public any more counterplans without due caution, [both I and] my whole family will on that account be punished.

However, the present shogun and the feudal lords are all like a bunch of drunks, and there is nothing that can be done to save them. Our only recourse is to place our hopes in dedicated lower-ranking people. We can by no means be unmindful of the kindness of this domain [Chōshū] and the goodness of the imperial court. Accordingly, if by means of such dedicated lower-ranking people we are able to give support first of all to this domain and next aid in the restoration of the Court, though it at first glance seems to violate the spirit of allegiance of individuals, still, anyone who does such things [i.e., plans and puts them into effect] can be said to have rendered meritorious service on behalf of the Divine Country. Such a man would be a greater person than even Kuang Chung [an illustrious minister in ancient China].

What is the situation of the foreign barbarians? In my opinion, the handling of the Americans seems to be proceeding smoothly. The founding ideals of America are splendid and the nation itself is not very old. I think it is our most formidable enemy. As for the English, many members of the domain have gone to Nagasaki and then exaggerated the weakness of the English. The Russians have a large-country spirit, but they seem to be a little careless. What is your opinion?

Even among the Americans there are some I do not fear; Harris, who came to Edo Castle, is one. There are an extremely large number of lies in what he says. Yet the fact that no one in the shogunate has been able to get the better of him in an argument is truly deplorable. If everything Harris says were to be put into effect, the Divine Country would really be in danger. If his words are only empty threats, we could not be more fortunate. What do you think? Since the Americans have no territories in the East, it is inevitable that they desire Java or Japan.

These are my thoughts; I have not been able to explain each of them in detail. To sum up, the way things stand now the Divine Country's downfall is certain. To restore it, some Liu Pang [first emperor of the Han dynasty], Hsiang Yu [pre-Han general] or Napoleon is absolutely necessary. Yet no one has paid any attention to this matter. Since you always have singular opinions and rare knowledge, I would like to hear your views.

11

MAKI IZUMI

Record of a Great Dream

November 18, 1859

A third response to Ii Naosuke's decision to sign a commercial treaty with the United States and purge officials who disagreed with him came from a Shinto priest in Kyushu. Unlike Yoshida Shōin, who placed his trust in the revolutionary potential of the common man (Document 10), Maki Izumi (1813–1864) dreamed of making the emperor into a charismatic figure capable of leading an army against the Tokugawa. At a time when even the emperor still believed that with proper guidance the Tokugawa shoguns should handle political affairs and international relations, this document issued one of the first calls for direct imperial rule.

Maki was born into a family of Shinto priests in the Kurume domain, whose shrine, the Suitengū, had close enough ties to the imperial court that Maki was granted court rank and the honorific title of Izumi (the name of one of Japan's provinces). He studied ancient Japanese history and Japanese classical poetry but focused his attention on the writings of the Mito School, especially those of Aizawa Seishisai (Document 1). Like many activists, Maki responded to the arrival of foreign envoys by developing a passionate attachment to imperial loyalism as a means of rescuing Japan from barbarian defilement. After Yoshida Shōin's death, Maki became a leader of the loyalist cause and worked with several of Shōin's disciples, including Kusaka Genzui and Takasugi Shinsaku. In 1864 he fought and died alongside Chōshū samurai in a failed attempt to take possession of the imperial palace in Kyoto (Document 19).

Seething with rage, the emperor suddenly summoned his ministers: "Some things are bearable, but others are not. There are matters on which I, as Emperor, must speak."

The ministers replied: "Humbly we obey. We will instruct the shogun's envoy to appear before you."

Bakushaku Arima-ke Shūshisho, ed., *Maki Izumi ibun* (Tokyo: Maki Yasuomi Sensei Kenshōkai, 1913). Translated by M. William Steele.

A secret message from the emperor was dispatched [to sympathetic lords]:

"Puny though I may be, I welcome the demands of my office. Not wishing to bring shame upon my ancestors, day and night I exert myself to the utmost. It was on this basis that I ascended the throne.

"When I received word that the Western barbarians had violated our divine land, I sent an imperial rescript to the shogunate requesting it to make defense preparations. However, the officials took their time and accomplished little. This led to the crisis of 1853. Since then, many foreign ships have arrived at our shores. Their intrusion has, in the end, resulted in great harm.

"At this point, heaven and earth and gods and devils alike began to issue ominous warnings. The earth shook and the seas raged. A comet appeared as a harbinger of doom. Since then every year has witnessed some form of disaster. Nonetheless, the shogun's officers have not awakened to the urgency of the problem. When it came to the winter of 1857, as could be expected, the barbarians demanded the impossible. The officials should have known that this would be their intention. I gave the officials instructions, advising them to reject the requests [to allow trade]. Courteously, I urged them upon this course of action. However, I have learned that my words were ignored, and instead the shogunate granted the barbarians' requests. Only afterward was I informed of this decision. Despite my anger that the officials, out of fear of the barbarians, had disregarded my instructions, I graciously assented to what they had done.

"In order to gather intelligence, I ordered the Tokugawa shogun and his close relatives to discuss matters with the great lords of the land. However, even though the shogun met with his related lords, they had already imprisoned all those who opposed their views.

"Moreover, they used flimsy excuses to choose the youngest candidate to become the next shogun.[1] His youth meant that he would meekly follow the officials' instructions. If by some chance these actions do not destroy the shogunate, they may well destroy the realm. The Tokugawa family has abandoned its obligations.

"It is my wish, as emperor, to travel to the east in order to inquire into these crimes. I ask you and your men to join me in a military campaign. I do not require a large number of soldiers. Rather I ask for unquestioning loyalty and passion. Will we not present a magnificent sight?

---

[1] Tokugawa Iemochi was thirteen years old when he assumed office in 1858.

"At a certain date, everyone should gather at Kyoto and await instructions. Ise, Bizen, Inaba, Chōshū, and Tosa should each send one squadron; Hizen and Higo, Chikuzen and Chikugo, and Satsuma should each send two. An envoy should be sent to Kaga, instructing [the daimyo] to assume command of lesser lords from the subsidiary domains of Yonezawa and Shinano. I will proceed to Usui [a mountain pass near Karuizawa]."

Such was the text of the imperial rescript.

"Sendai domain, moreover, is ordered to lead troops from the Akita, Nihonmatsu, Takasaki, and Mihara domains. I, the Emperor, will proceed to Tsunekuni [in present-day Toyama Prefecture]."

This too was in accordance with the imperial rescript.

The various lords assembled in Kyoto, where the emperor informed them of their divine mission. The Imperial Prince, he said, would take charge of the government in Kyoto while he led the expedition. The prince would be assisted by certain lords and nobles, among whom would be the lords of Satsuma and Chikuzen domains. The lord of Ise domain commanded the first squad of advance troops. Bizen followed and Inaba came next.

The imperial guard consisted of Tosa domain on the left wing and Yonezawa domain on the right. Higo domain assumed the rear. This organization was determined in advance. On the march, they arrived first at Ise Shrine, where they made prayers and offerings, before proceeding to the Atsuta Grand Shrine, where they venerated the imperial sword [one of the three imperial treasures]. Afterward, the troops proceeded [in the direction of Edo]. They cleared the way through the barrier at Hakone so that camp could be made at Tōfukuji temple. Advance troops set up camp at Odawara and Yumoto. The left and right wings of the army and the rear guard set up camp in Yamanaka Castle in Mishima. Afterward, they dispatched envoys to inform the shogun's chief adviser, Ii Naosuke, his consort, road guards, and officials [of the impending campaign]. The shogun's ranking ministers, along with the lords present [in Edo], were ordered to assemble in submission. Ii Naosuke withdrew into the courtyard to await orders; his consort arrived later in procession. The emperor carefully oversaw everything and made sure there would be no betrayal.

The shogun's officials suffered a severe scolding. Afterward, they were told to withdraw to Yamanaka Castle. The troops to the left, right, and rear served as guard. Prior to this, the emperor himself admonished the lords in Edo, and his officials demanded obedience from the lords in charge of Edo Castle and Osaka Castle. All of the shogun's officials were placed under imperial control and forbidden to move around without permission. Edo city officials took their orders from the imperial command. Assemblies and demonstrations were prohibited.

The emperor reprimanded and demoted the young shogun Iemochi, giving him fief lands in Kai and Suruga, where he became the chief, with troops belonging to those domains placed under his control. With headquarters in Osaka Castle, the Imperial Prince was appointed to the position of shogun, charged with the pacification of the eastern domains, and given command of other troops from domains [formerly loyal to the Tokugawa family]. Lords possessed of exceptional talent were made into commanding generals and moved to the Kawagoe and Kanazawa domains; the size of their fiefs was increased to 100,000 *koku*.[2] The lord of Nihonmatsu domain was transferred to Kazusa and the size of his fief was increased to 150,000 *koku*. All of these lords were placed in charge of ports and coastal defense.

The imperial troops executed Ii Naosuke and his subordinates. The emperor took over Edo Castle and announced a great reform edict. The lords were instructed to remain in their residences, to learn if they would be called to imperial service. This happened ten days before the imperial progress. All men imprisoned by the shogunate and held in Owari, Mito, and Echizen were released and allowed to return to their homes.

An imperial guard was formed. It was sent to the north, by sea route to Sendai, from there to Echigo, and then on campaigns to Kaga, Echizen, Wakasa, and Tanba. Thereafter it proceeded to occupy and set up headquarters in Osaka Castle.

The imperial regime recognized men of talent. It forbade luxury and encouraged frugality. Taxes were lightened; service requirements were reduced. Schools were established in order to cultivate talent. The nation was made wealthy and the army strong. Trust and goodwill spread wide.

Areas of reform were far-reaching. Edo was transformed into the imperial capital. Domains were newly established and the administration of towns and villages reformed. Rites and music flourished. Gradually it all came to pass.

Such is the dream that came to me on the night of the 13th day of the 10th month of the 5th year of Ansei (November 18, 1859).

---

[2]One *koku* equaled 5.1 bushels of rice, enough to feed one man for a year. It constituted the standard measure of landed wealth in this period.

12

To Kill the Wicked

March 24, 1860

When the newly appointed chief senior councilor, Ii Naosuke, reasserted shogunal authority by signing a commercial treaty without imperial approval (Document 8), negotiating a series of treaties with other nations, and choosing Tokugawa Iemochi, a boy of thirteen with the best bloodline, to be the next shogun, his autocratic manner earned him many enemies. These included the supporters of Tokugawa Nariaki, along with outside daimyo such as the Satsuma lord from Kyushu, who felt excluded from national politics. To quell opposition, Ii imprisoned or executed his enemies in what became known as the Great Purge of the Ansei era (1854–1860).

Ii's strong-arm tactics eventually drove his opponents to violence. On March 24, 1860, just as shogunal ambassadors arrived in Washington, D.C., to ratify the new Treaty of Amity and Commerce, a band of seventeen samurai from Mito—joined by Arimura Jizaemon, a samurai from Satsuma—assassinated Ii as he was about to enter Edo Castle by the Sakurada Gate. This was an unprecedented attack on a high shogunal official. Arimura cut off Ii Naosuke's head but suffered severe wounds himself at the hands of Ii's attendants. The assassins justified their deed in a manifesto titled "To Kill the Wicked." One of the assassins, Sano Takenosuke, inscribed a poem on his undergarment to convey his thoughts. In the end, the samurai were surrounded. Arimura, Sano, and several others committed suicide on the spot. Those who surrendered were executed. It was clear to all, however, that the shogunate's authority had been severely tested.

Sometimes change in national policy is necessary, and conditions may arise making it difficult to avoid administrative reform; however, the measures undertaken by the shogunate after the American barbarians entered the Uraga Bay [in 1853] are completely unacceptable. With the

Mito-han shiryō, jō-henkan (Tokyo: Yoshikawa Kōbunkan, 1970), 816–17. For a summary translation, see H. Satoh, *Agitated Japan: The Life of Baron Ii Kamon-no-kami; Based on the* Kaikoku Shimatsu *of Shimada Saburo* (New York: Appleton, 1896), 137–40. Translated by M. William Steele.

excuse of preserving peace under the threat of war and fearing the barbarians' vacuous threats, the [shogun's] officers have negotiated [with Townsend Harris] over issues of trade and friendship, granted him entry to the castle and an audience [with Shogun Iesada], concluded a treaty, halted the practice of treading on the cross, allowed for the construction of temples of the evil religion, and permitted foreign ministers to reside permanently [in our country]. These acts have not only caused immutable harm to the martial values bequeathed to our divine land from ancient times, insulted our national honor, and betrayed the august teachings of our ancestors, but in failing to heed the imperial will, the shogunate has gravely insulted the imperial court. Truly, these are things that never should have happened.

When we look at the deeds of Ii Naosuke, the chief senior councilor, we see that he has taken advantage of the youth of the new shogun and arrogated power to himself. He refrains from open and just discussion. He has slandered and abused all those who work sincerely on behalf of the shogunate and the court, beginning with members of the close relatives of the Tokugawa family, and including members of the nobility, large and small daimyo, and direct retainers of the Tokugawa family. Some he has forced into retirement and others into confinement or prison. And yet, the barbarians are upon us like a plague. Day by day our alarm grows at the unsettled times upon us: trouble from within and threats from without. People's fears are so great and numerous that the heart of the emperor is consumed with grief. It has been his fervent desire to establish a permanent foundation for peace and security within the nation and unity between the imperial court and the shogunate. Knowing that the emperor's wish is to cast off the scorn displayed by the barbarians, entreaties were made to the emperor to prepare a rescript on national affairs. However, ignoring the emperor's concerns, false charges were brought against various lords and other men of high purpose. They were rounded up, imprisoned, and subjected to cruel punishment. Most heinous is the case of the three court nobles [Konoe, minister of the left; Takatsukasa, minister of the right, and Sanjō, minister of the left] who were forced to take the tonsure [making them Buddhist monks]. In addition, Prince Awataguchi of Shūrenin was placed in confinement. We have even heard that there are plans to request the emperor to abdicate. For such treacherous deeds, there is surely no remedy. Ii Naosuke is indeed an unpardonable enemy of the nation.

The crimes committed by Ii Naosuke are enumerated in detail in a separate statement. If such a tyrannical villain is left unfettered, the governing authority of the shogunate will increasingly become disordered and foreign barbarians will continue to menace our shores. The very existence of our nation is clearly at stake. Our indignation is such that we can no longer maintain our silence. To the emperor in Kyoto we report that we have consecrated ourselves to be the instruments of heavenly punishment and will seek to execute this wicked man. Our conduct, however, does not indicate the slightest enmity to the government of the shogun. Rather, our action is motivated solely by the holy and wise will of the emperor to restore the government of the shogun to its proper form, to revere the emperor and expel the barbarians, to promote the way of justice, fraternity, and wisdom, and to create a national unity of all people on a basis as firm and unmovable as Mount Fuji itself. We are determined to die for our country and seek to repay the debt we owe the emperor. This we swear before heaven and earth, gods and men.

Poem by Sano Takenosuke, One of the Men from Mito

Hold aloft the imperial brocade banner of Japan
Send forth the army of our august Emperor
Fallen petals and bodies of the dead may be scattered at Sakurada
But there is no stopping the Yamato spirit![1]

[1]"Yamato" is an old term for Japan, often used in combination with other words to emphasize that the speaker and his audience are uniquely Japanese.

13

TSUKIOKA YOSHITOSHI

Woodblock Print of the 1860 Assassination of Ii Naosuke at Sakurada Gate

1874

On the snowy morning of March 24, 1860, the shogun's chief senior councilor, Ii Naosuke, headed for the Sakurada Gate outside Edo Castle, surrounded by an entourage of sixty men. Waiting near the gate were seventeen samurai from Mito and one from Satsuma. They attacked so quickly that before Ii's attendants had time to unwrap their swords from the capes that protected them from the snow, the assassins had killed Ii by thrusting their swords into his palanquin. In the fight that followed, a number of men on both sides died.

The incident shocked and fascinated the Edo populace. It attracted throngs of sightseers, who interrogated bystanders, and the men who survived the attack gave their versions of the event as well. In this gorgeously colored 1874 print, Tsukioka Yoshitoshi (1839–1892), famous for his graphic depictions of violence and death, leaves no doubt that the road to the Meiji Restoration was a bloody one. At the center is Sano Takenosuke, a pro-imperial samurai from Mito. He is clutching the assassins' manifesto (Document 12) in one hand as he grapples with Ii's attendants. The light-colored captions name the Mito samurai; Ii's attendants have dark colored captions. To increase the scene's drama, Yoshitoshi shows a much more spirited defense of the palanquin than Ii's retainers were able to achieve.

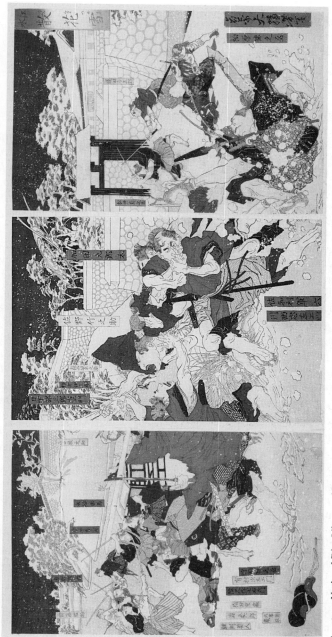

Courtesy National Diet Library of Japan.

81

14

YOKOI SHŌNAN

The Three Major Problems of State Policy
1860

In 1860, shortly after Ii Naosuke's assassination and his failed attempt to strengthen the shogunate, Yokoi Shōnan (1809–1869) gave a series of lectures on the range of political, economic, and cultural problems that Japan faced as a result of contact with the West. Originally from Kumamoto, in Kyushu, Yokoi served as a political adviser to Matsudaira Yoshinaga, the daimyo of Fukui, who was an advocate of a more public distribution of political responsibility than the Tokugawa shogunate afforded.

Yokoi recommended three areas of reform: economic, military, and spiritual. He began with a critique of the Tokugawa seclusion policy, which he described as a disservice to Japan's political and economic health. While it served the private interests of the Tokugawa family, it failed to advance national interests. Yokoi went on to contrast Japan's "lack of government" with the situation in Western countries. In his eyes, America could serve as the model for domestic political and economic reform. He was particularly impressed with George Washington, who was responsible, he concluded, for making America into the most enlightened nation in the world. Yokoi stressed the need for determined and drastic change. Military reform, particularly the creation of a national navy, was a priority. In contrast with the xenophobia displayed by Aizawa Seishisai (Document 1), Yokoi Shōnan's plan for renovation sought not only to unite the hearts of all Japanese but also to give them the confidence to become active and respected members of international society.

[Evils of Seclusion]

After the American mission submitted its state letter proposing friendship and trade in the summer of 1853, the shogunate invited the opinions of the feudal lords on the question of accepting or rejecting these

Yokoi Shōnan, "Kokuze Sanron: The Three Major Problems of State Policy," trans. and with notes by D. Y. Miyauchi, *Monumenta Nipponica* 23, nos. 1/2 (1968): 157–60, 167–69, 174–76.

proposals. Thereafter, the various pros and cons over foreign trade were argued, but no solution could be reached. . . . Let us examine the merits of the two opposing views. First, from the side of the seclusionists, the drawbacks of trade are as follows:

1. Because our land was productive in the five grains, in gold and silver, and in a multitude of things, and because the people did not lack anything in carrying out their livelihood, we did not know even the slightest want during the centuries of seclusion. However, if we now open up our locked doors, useful things will leave our country, and unnecessary things will be brought in.

2. If the volume of exports is large, there will be a shortage of necessary things in our country.

3. As a consequence of the shortage of necessities, prices will greatly increase.

4. Those who profit from this trade are the merchants involved whereas the whole nation suffers.

5. Even if goods are to be exchanged for gold and silver, there is no sense in exchanging necessities, which will become scarce, for gold and silver, of which there has been an adequate amount since earlier times.

Already because of foreign trade, prices of goods have risen, to the detriment of all four classes of people, and hard times are virtually at hand. These are the harmful effects of trade.

. . . The harmful effects of national seclusion are given next. Since our seclusion has become a deeply rooted practice of over 200 years, its evils are great indeed, yet people are not aware of them as being injurious. Let us examine the reasons for this.

The period of 200 years ago was preceded by an era of internal strife, and consequently all things including clothing, food and housing were frugal and plain. Compared to the period of wars, the lives of the people were settled, and therefore there were no complaints. However, the long years of peace were naturally followed by a trend towards luxuries. The style of living of the daimyo throughout Japan gradually became that of sumptuous formality. The expenditures of silver and gold for various uses, including the system of attendance in Edo, increased, whereas the population grew but the land area remained unchanged. Consumption increased while production became inadequate. People of lower ranks followed the pattern of living of the daimyo, while the moneyed people, forgetting their social status, indulged in extravagances. Even the people of little means ignored their circumstances in their efforts to follow along. As a result everyone was reduced to distress. Furthermore pleasure seekers and idlers, basking in the benefits of peace, multiplied to a ratio of nine out of every ten persons.

With the number of producers the same as before but with a great increase in the number of consumers, the prices of goods naturally rose. With the rise in prices, the supply of gold and silver became insufficient. And the shortage of gold and silver created hardships for all four classes of people. The peasant, artisan and merchant classes lived by their labor, however, and the value of their labor increased along with the value of their products; hence, they were able to make ends meet. The samurai, including the daimyo, on the other hand, were limited in their income, so when their expenses surpassed this limit, there was simply no ready solution.

Under the feudal system during the period of national seclusion, the various daimyo isolated their own provinces, or counties, without considering the harm to others so long as there was gain for themselves. Despite the fact that there was not a single case of a government that did not seek profit, it was difficult to supplement the deficiencies for state expenditures. Hence, inevitably the stipends of the samurai were withheld in the form of loans, money was squeezed from rich farmers and merchants, and the lifeblood of the common people was sucked. Even with these measures the emergency of the present day cannot be remedied.

Because farmers and merchants become impoverished, eventually they try to escape from their distress by raising prices, thereby extending the suffering to the samurai. The distinctions in honors and etiquette between high and low become blurred, and people become disrespectful. It is not rare for people to rise up and to press upon their superiors with complaints about their distress. With the accumulation of these incidents over the years, inevitably riots take place. In an effort to remedy this evil, economies are widely carried out by eliminating things which are not beneficial—including the inessentials in clothing, food and housing—and adding only the useful. What will happen is that first the inessentials will be eliminated; then, if that does not suffice, essentials will be cut out. When that happens, that which should be paid cannot be given. When the government through its own economies is at last able to rescue its immediate financial needs, it has no margin left to aid the samurai. The samurai class in an effort to escape from its straitened circumstances through economies of its own may attempt to return to the old frugal ways by severe decrees, tearing down luxury houses and discarding fine clothes.

However, not only is it difficult to change suddenly the ways which have become firmly accepted, but luxuries have become so commonplace that they are no longer thought of as luxuries. On the contrary, economies are considered as new decrees of cruel hardship. People do not understand the beneficial decrees. They want to indulge in their extravagant ways even though they suffer. Therefore, because of human weakness, they resist. . . .

Today with all nations navigating freely and trading with each other like neighbors, if Japan alone holds on tightly to its seclusion law, it will be unable to escape the armed might of foreign enemies. When that happens it is extremely doubtful that the state can be administered, let alone make adequate military preparations, with national power virtually lacking, nor rally the samurai and commoners—some resisting, others resentful—into setting up a policy of defense, and driving out the foreigners.

These are the evils of seclusion. . . .

[The Western Model]

In our country from the middle ages wars have followed in succession, the Imperial Court has become weak, and various lords have parceled out groups of provinces, each defending his own territory while attacking others in turn. The people were looked upon as so much waste, and the severity of forced labor and the arbitrary collection of military rations knew no bounds. Good government was swept away from the land, and it was a period in which one who was skilled in warfare became a great lord and one who was clever in planning became a renowned minister.

Consequently in the early seventeenth century when a period of peace had come, these old ways remained. The great retainers on the war council, including Honda Masanobu (1538–1616), all strove to make the foundation of the Tokugawa household supreme and firm, and not once was consideration given to the people of the realm. Although there are said to have been many outstanding rulers and ministers from that time to the present, all have continued the work of administering the private affairs of one household only. The various lords have followed this pattern, and according to the old ways handed down from their ancestors, they have planned with their ministers for the convenience and security of their own provinces with a barrier between neighboring provinces.

As a result, those who are known as great ministers in the shogunate and in the provinces have not all been able to disentangle themselves from the old ways of national seclusion. They have devoted themselves to their lords and their provinces, while their feelings of love and loyalty for the most part ignore the virtues of the good life and on the contrary invite the resentment of the people. All this leads to troubles in ruling the land. Japan has been split up thusly and lacks a unified system. Therefore we must admit that Envoy Perry's observation in his *Expedition to Japan* about the lack of government machinery in Japan when he arrived here in 1854 was truly a discerning one. . . .

Under the system of national seclusion Japan sought safety in isolation. Hence it experienced no wars or defeats. However, the world situation has undergone vast changes. Each country has broadly developed enlightened government.

In America three major policies have been set up from Washington's presidency on: First, to stop wars in accordance with divine intentions, because nothing is worse than violence and killing among nations; second, to broaden enlightened government by learning from all the countries of the world; and third, to work with complete devotion for the peace and welfare of the people by entrusting the power of the president of the whole country to the wisest instead of transmitting it to the son of the president. . . . All methods of administrative laws and practices and all men who are known as good and wise throughout the world are put into the country's service and a very beneficial administration—one not completely in the interest of the rulers—is developed.

In England the government is based entirely on the popular will, and all government actions—large and small—are always debated by the people. The most beneficial action is decided upon, and an unpopular program is not forced upon the people. War or peace is decided thusly. When there were wars lasting several years against Russia and against China at a huge cost in men and money, all taken from the people, not one person complained against them. Furthermore, all countries, including Russia, have established schools and military academies, hospitals, orphanages, and schools for the deaf and dumb. The governments are entirely based on moral principles, and they work hard for the benefit of the people, virtually as in the three ancient periods when the virtuous sage kings [celebrated as the originators of Chinese civilization] ruled China.

Thus when the various countries attempt to open Japan's doors according to the way of international cooperation, who would not call Japan a fool for persisting in its old seclusionist views, for ruling for the benefit of private interests, and for not knowing the principles of commercial intercourse? . . .

[The Call for a National Navy]

This year English and French forces have attacked the Manchu empire, taking Tientsin and pressing on to the capital at Peking. Russia is watching from the sidelines to take advantage of a stalemate and is like a tiger waiting to pounce on its prey. If Russia has designs of dominating China, then a great force must be mustered to prevent this. England must also be feared.

With the situation beyond the seas like this and growing worse all the time, how can Japan arouse its martial vigor when it alone basks in peace and comfort and drills its indolent troops as though it were child's play? Because there is no navy a defense policy simply does not exist. . . .

Japan is an island country off the east coast of Asia, just as England is to Europe. Because the surrounding seas are rough and because of the dread of the rise of violent winds, navigation is extremely difficult. Hence there has been no attack by foreign invaders. Shikoku and Kyushu are set off by water, thus facilitating transportation. Products are abundant, so it is not necessary to seek anything abroad. With what good design did the creator form such a favorable land? The Japanese people are indeed fortunate to be born in such a blessed nation. . . .

But as we have discussed above, the situation in foreign countries has greatly changed with rapid advances in navigation. Traffic on the oceans is now more convenient and faster than on land. Since the invention of the steamship, distant lands have become like neighbors. Outside of the polar seas there is no place on earth that cannot be reached. When even natural hazards are no longer a hindrance to navigation, Japan is no longer in the situation in which it alone can seclude itself.

For several decades Russia had been requesting permission for trade in vain. England's requests also had been rejected. Therefore America long and carefully laid out plans, and in 1853 its warships entered Uraga Bay, and bluffing with its armed might it eventually unlocked our closed doors. Thereafter the Russians, English and French came in succession and set up procedures for peaceful trade.

Japan has consequently gained some information on the conditions beyond the seas. However, we still cling to our antiquated views and depend on our skill in hand-to-hand fighting. Some believe that we can quickly learn to fire in rifle formations and thus avert indignities. Indeed, our outmoded practices are pitiable.

Today the islands of Japan are like a great ship, and the four seas are like land. If we defend against foreign navies with our armies, that would be like fighting land warfare from a ship. They would be like the host, and we, the guest. It would be difficult for us to advance in attack, while there would be no place for us to retreat to in defense. They could advance when they saw an advantage, or retreat when it was unfavorable. Because they could advance and retreat freely, we could be forced into action, but we could not take the initiative. Furthermore if they should appear with two or three warships, we must defend our entire seacoast. We would be exhausted by the fruitless and ceaseless activity and be defeated without a battle.

Moreover, they can by being in our home waters interfere with and seize our shipping. With the routes of our whole nation cut, our difficulties would be enormous. A city like Edo would be starved within a few days. Just by considering these few problems we can see that an army is not important but that we must build up a navy.

When we consider England, it prevents indignities being committed by foreigners, and it rules possessions. Without its armed power it would be unable to maintain its prestige. . . . Today it has over 700 steam navy ships, 88,000 fighting men, and 240 armored warships. Compared to former times there are twice as many fighting men. . . . The circumstances of Japan and England are very much alike, and therefore our militarization should be patterned after that of England, with 420 navy ships, 15,000 cannons, 29,500 sailors, 13,000 fighting men and 900 officers in the navy. Military camps must be set up in the areas of our open ports, and warships must be stationed there in preparation for emergencies. They can go to each other's assistance when circumstances require, and they should be adequate to forestall any indignities. England is situated in the northwest, and its land is not good. But with the advantages of a maritime country, it has seized distant territories and has become a great power today.

Better yet, Japan lies in the central part of the earth, and we excel in the advantages of a sea environment. If the shogunate should issue a new decree and stir up the characteristic vigor and bravery of the Japanese and unite the hearts of the entire nation with a firmly established military system based on clarified laws, not only is there no need to fear foreign countries, but we can sail to various lands within a few years, and even if the latter should unloosen armed attacks, we can with our moral principles and courage be looked up to for our benevolent ways.

15

Reform of Relations between Shogun and Daimyo

June–October 1862

Beset on all sides, the shogunate tried to repair its relations with the court by having Princess Kazunomiya marry the shogun in return for a promise to expel the barbarians. When that did not work, in June 1862 the shogun's senior councilors decided that they needed to institute a new series of reforms to renew the government. The first of these so-called Bunkyū reforms aimed at streamlining administration and cutting costs, in part by encouraging aged retainers to retire. The second and most famous reform, which came about only after months of debate and a well-timed memorial (a written statement offered to his lord) by Yokoi Shōnan, reduced the requirements for daimyo to spend time in Edo. If daimyo spent less time and money on traveling back and forth to Edo to pay homage to the shogun, they would have more to devote to national defense. They even received permission to buy warships from foreigners.

Allowing the daimyo to take their wives and heirs back to their domains destroyed the hostage system that for over two centuries had guaranteed their loyalty to the shogun. When the shogun decided that he had to go to Kyoto to meet with the emperor, the visit exposed his inability to control policy. Although the shogun's advisers hoped that their reforms would enhance the shogunate's domination of national affairs, the twin goals of a stronger shogunate and a stronger national defense ultimately proved to be incompatible.

June 21, 1862: Announcement by Inaba Masami to the Senior Inspector and Inspectors

For all the military units, the guards, and the police forces to practice drill in Western guns and cannon with special diligence, the military training center, Etchūjima, and other places in Edo are too confined, a pale shadow of the reality of the battlefield. Therefore the members

---

Suzuki Tōzo and Koike Shōtarō, eds., *Fujiokaya nikki*, vol. 10 (Tokyo: San'ichi Shobō, 1991), 356, 357, 367; Tokutomi Choichirō (Sōho), *Bunkyū taisei ichihen*, vol. 2, *Kinsei Nihon kokuminshi* (Tokyo: Min'yūsha, 1936), 165–66; Nihon shiseki kyōkai, ed., *Zokusaimu kiji 1*, vol. 106 of *Nihon shiseki kyōkai sōsho* (Tokyo: Tōkyō Daigaku Shuppankai, 1921, 1974), 51–55. Translated by Anne Walthall.

of these units and the foot soldiers with their commanders on horse-back are all to line up in procession and go to the area of Tokumaru in Musashi for drills. It is all right for them to spend the night there depending on the weather, but you are to make sure that there is no lack of supervision.

You are to make sure that the troops are kept in line in leaving the city.

June 19, 1862: Shogunal Statement

Given the current relations with foreign countries, we must fully commit ourselves to military preparations, plan reforms in accord with the times, and return to a simpler system and the honest, plain ways of the samurai. Everyone must thoroughly understand this and encourage loyal service for our military spirit to shine forth.

June 27, 1862: Directive by Senior Councilors

During almost three hundred years of peace, evil customs have spread, official discipline has relaxed, and we have not been attentive to military preparedness. Recently we have repeatedly gotten embroiled in foreign affairs, the way these have been handled has naturally reverberated throughout the realm, and we are horrified that all of this has caused the emperor anguish. In the beginning, there was not the slightest estrangement between court and military, but somehow or other we are no longer able to communicate. Therefore the shogun intends to go to Kyoto immediately, where he wants to report everything directly to the emperor, and this has already been announced privately.

The ritual for the shogun to go to Kyoto having fallen into oblivion ever since the Kan'ei era (1624–1644), it would be difficult to rush a thorough investigation of all the precedents, and the elders petitioned for a little bit of leeway. However, there are no precedents for the current state of affairs. Since it is our intention that as much ceremony as possible be omitted, and attire on the road and so forth be as simple as possible, a quick investigation is all that is needed. This is something that the shogun has decided on very quickly, so you should sincerely take everything into consideration and report to him directly. Given our combined and firm resolve, our united military authority will banish evil customs. While making our imperial nation rank with the world's first-class powers, we intend that through our great achievements we will bring tranquility to the eternal emperor's mind above, and below we will have the common people live in peace.

October 15, 1862: To the Daimyo

You are to be given a relaxation in the terms of your service to the shogun. If you have any ideas concerning the success or failure, rights or wrongs, in the policy taken by the government's administration, these are to be stated in full when you pay your visits to the castle during your stay in Edo. Furthermore you should then make inquiries or statements regarding the pros and cons of local governance, plans for installing defenses on land and sea, and so forth. All of the daimyo are to consult together on these matters. Indeed, the shogun will question you directly regarding these matters.

Although the rotation of the number of men assigned to the capital is as given on a separate sheet of paper, if you are retiring, if there be pre-existing conditions, or if there be an unavoidable necessity, you may depart the capital.

Heirs may reside wherever they please, whether in the capital, in the domain, or in a village.

When you move to your domain, the retainers permanently stationed in Edo may be granted leave upon submission of a petition. You should give instructions for the duties to be allotted to them based on the schedule for your stays in Edo given on a separate sheet of paper.

Concerning your wives and children resident here, you may take them back to your domain or not as you please. You are also free to have your children stay in the capital in order for them to understand the current situation.

Few retainers need to be stationed in your compounds here when you are absent. The compounds should be kept as simple as possible with the understanding that they are merely an inn or a government outpost for your visits to the capital. Furthermore, aside from armaments, all the useless furnishings are to be curtailed. It is all right for your retainers to dress in nothing but traveling clothes, even if they are serving at the head of your retinue or as messengers.

There will soon be instructions concerning the defense of places distant from domains [that this will no longer be required].

Offerings such as the money paid in lieu of swords and horses at the first of the year and the eight seasonal ceremonies, as well as for the ceremonies of coming to Edo for service to the shogun, succession to headship, and others, are to continue as they have up to now. However, in the case of goods that are a bother to procure, you may petition to change to something else. . . .

Since at this time a relaxation is ordered in the rate at which all the daimyo come to serve the shogun in Edo, daimyo who are supposed to come to the capital this year may either stay in their domain or return there, regardless of whether they have postponed their trip because of illness or are already on the road.

Those with holdings above 10,000 *koku* are permitted to ride on horseback all the way up to the castle if they so choose. Inside the palace, they are to wear ordinary *hakama* or *hakama* cut high enough to ride a horse [instead of ceremonial pants that trail behind them].

Inside the castle they are to reduce the number of their attendants as much as possible. . . .

Now that officials have received orders to reduce their retinues and all of the houses in the capital have shrunk their staffs, there will be previously employed foot soldiers, mid-level servants, and others resident among the townspeople who will be fired. Many people who left their ancestral villages to spend years serving in military households have no discernible skills, and because they will suffer hardships to suddenly lose their livelihood, there is no way for them to put their affairs in order here. People who petition to return to their ancestral villages will receive allowances, and we will summon intendants from the shogunate's lands, officials from the shogun's lands held in trust, retainers from lords holding more than 10,000 *koku*, or retainers or village officials from fief holders with less than 10,000 *koku* or from temple or shrine lands to turn the individuals over to them to be escorted home. They are then to be turned over to their local officials and relatives to be returned to farming. People who cannot do farming are to be sent back to their wives or else put to work in the mountains or on the sea, and they are to be given every assistance so that they can live securely in their ancestral villages.

16

Woodblock Print: "The Way Things Are Now"
1863

The year 1863 was a difficult one for the citizens of Edo. Among the problems they faced was the fear that war might follow the murder of Englishman Charles Richardson on September 14, 1862, for showing disrespect to the Satsuma regent. This fear was exacerbated by surges in commodity prices owing to foreigners buying up gold, increases in petty theft, the assassination of foreigners and merchants who dealt in foreign goods, and the sudden displacement of people after the daimyo moved their families and retainers back to their home domains (Document 15). So-called panic prints were produced in great numbers in order to satisfy the desire of people wanting to understand current events. The print reproduced here includes information on "the way things are now."

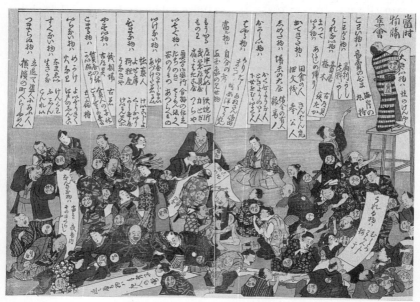

Courtesy of Hachiro Yuasa Memorial Museum, International Christian University.

The Way Things Are Now

What's important? Being frugal.

Who's scared? Shop owners forced to close. Rich people living near the coast.

What should we be frightened of? Moneylenders. Pawnshops.

What can't be sold? Shopping stalls. Used goods. Potted plants and flowers.

Who's funny? Cowards. Foolhardy people. Anyone wanting to employ a maid.

What's popular? Flophouses. Shimada hairdos [an elaborate hairstyle for women]. Western lamps.

What's a hit? Thinking for oneself. Seeing the elephant at Ryōgoku.

Who's making money? Cheap roadside eats. Gun shops. Military goods stores. Sword sharpeners. Wicker trunk sellers.

What's cheap? The exchange rate for copper coins. Used clothing. Antiques.

What's distressing? Pawnshops taking a day off. Poor people's children. Cat snatchers. Dirty old men. Hemorrhoids.

What's in short supply? Unadulterated food and drink. Brawls. Fresh fish. Construction. Weddings.

What's not worth noticing? People who get robbed. Yokohama merchants. Cheap prostitutes.

Who's in a fix? Landlords. Night peddlers. Day laborers.

Hachiro Yuasa Memorial Museum, International Christian University. Translated by M. William Steele.

4

Radical Resistance

17

A Manifesto to Punish Traitors

April 10, 1863

A wave of assassinations terrorized Kyoto nobles and officials in the months between the shogun's announcement in September 1862 that he would visit the city the following spring and his arrival at the end of April 1863. The assassins, who called themselves shishi *(men of high purpose), killed the servants of men accused of disrespecting the throne by advocating Princess Kazunomiya's marriage to the shogun. They even threatened the shogun's guardian, Hitotsubashi Yoshinobu, by placing a severed head in front of the temple where he was staying. The message they sent was clear: Traitors deserved death.*

Among the people who flocked to Kyoto to try to assist the emperor were members of the Hirata Atsutane (1776–1843) School of Japanese history and native ways. Some were samurai, but others were shrine priests or merchants, connected only by their common affiliation with Atsutane. They, too, roamed the city, meeting with people of like mind and lamenting the shogun's unwillingness to expel the barbarians. When they realized that the mortuary temple for the Ashikaga shoguns (the predecessors of the Tokugawa) was near the house rented by Atsutane's son Kanetane, they decided to decapitate the first three shoguns' statues and display the heads on the banks of the Kamo River to convey a historically based warning to traitors.

Yoshida Tsunekichi and Satō Seizaburō, eds., *Bakumatsu seiji ronshū*, vol. 56 of *Nihon shisō taikei*, (Tokyo: Iwanami Shoten, 1976), 293–94. Translated by Anne Walthall.

Traitors: Ashikaga Takauji [1305–1358]
Ashikaga Yoshiakira [1330–1367]
Ashikaga Yoshimitsu [1358–1408]

It is now the time to rectify names and functions. We should investigate and punish all the disloyal retainers since the Kamakura period [1180–1333] one by one. Since these three traitors did the worst evil, their vile statues have been visited with the punishment of heaven. These heads are to remain exposed for three days. Anyone removing them will certainly be punished.

April 1863

The treachery of these men, having been discussed by the sages and made well known to all, hardly needs repeating today, but even though decapitating these statues at this time is therefore redundant, it will provide a glimpse of their crimes. Fundamental to the great way of our great country are the two words *utmost loyalty*. Contrary to the manners and customs in place since the age of the gods, when the forerunner in treachery, Yoritomo [1147–1199] of Kamakura, appeared, he distressed the court and began the practice of disloyalty. Thereafter when we get to the Hōjō [1199–1333] and the Ashikaga [1336–1573], their crimes and evil deeds should not have been permitted by heaven or earth, and they should have been punished with death by gods and men. Nevertheless, in a world in which the realm was in confusion because names of offices did not match their functions, the court had become so weak that it could not rectify these crimes. This is so regrettable, how can we not wail?

Seeing now the things the Ashikaga left behind, we are unable to restrain our rage. Thinking that unworthy though we are, had we lived five hundred years ago, we would have wrung their heads off, we are unable to stop clenching our fists and gnashing our teeth even for a moment. Now with the return to the past in all things and the current of the times running toward bringing about a complete change in old abuses, we have the opportunity at last to rectify the crimes committed by disloyal retainers. Therefore we agreed to punish the great crimes of these traitors. Last night, in order to clarify the great cause of duty, we removed the statues of those nasty bastards—Takauji, his son, and grandson—from Tōji-in where they were held, decapitated them, and exposed their heads in order to dispel even a little of the long-standing, ancient rage.

April 10, 1863

The great general Oda Nobunaga [1534–1582] wiped out the great criminal gangs, and it must be said that conditions improved a little.

However, from that time to now many people have surpassed these traitors. There are so many of them that their crimes exceed those of the Ashikaga and the others. If they do not repent these ancient evils, loyally expunge the evil customs existing since the Kamakura period, return to ancient ways by offering service to the court, and make up for their accumulated crimes, then all the loyalists in the realm will rise up together and punish them for their crimes.

April 10, 1863

18

MATSUO TASEKO

Lamenting the Useless Body of a Weak Woman

1864

Kyoto became a magnet in 1862, drawing people from all walks of life who sensed that it was becoming the center of power. Freed from attendance on the shogun, activist daimyo either went to Kyoto or sent spies there to keep them informed of what was happening. The shogun's supporters thronged the city once he announced that he would visit in the spring of 1863 to pay his respects to the emperor. Young men swarmed the streets, advocating reverence to the emperor, with the goal of promoting national cohesion by manifesting kokutai, *the national essence, as immutable as heaven and earth. They also signaled the need for national defense by calling for the expulsion of barbarians. Worthy aims, but difficult to achieve without a power base.*

Among these men was Matsuo Taseko (1811–1894), a farm woman from central Japan who came to Kyoto, she said, to study poetry, the literary medium considered most appropriate for women. A disciple of Hirata Atsutane, she also acted as a spy, using connections with court women to gain entry to the imperial palace. Implicated in the decapitation of the Ashikaga shoguns' statues (Document 17), she was forced to flee the city. Back home, she sent the following poem to a friend who shared her thoughts. It is a lament for both herself as a woman and the exiled disciples, unable to take meaningful action to aid the emperor.

Anne Walthall, *The Weak Body of a Useless Woman: Matsuo Taseko and the Meiji Restoration* (Chicago: University of Chicago Press, 1998), 227, 229–31.

A Long Poem Relating My Thoughts

What use am I as a person appearing
In the visible world
Governed by the gods through the emperor?

If I were a man
    In my left hand I would grasp
    A straight bow from Shinano where the fine bamboo is cut
    I would carry a straight sword at my hips
    I would forget my family and consider my life to be less than
       nothing.

Even though I am not worthy to be counted
    Among the mighty warriors
    Who go out to serve on that way
    Graced with the departed souls of the imperial ancestors
    I shout bravely to enflame true Japanese hearts.

People who know not the way
    The warriors from the boondocks
    Who incline their hearts to dwell in Yokohama,
    I say drive them all out
    Down to the last despicable savage.

From the bottom of my heart
    I am filled with ardor, but as you can see
    I grieve not knowing what to do
    Like the leech child unable to stand on its own
    And I am here to apologize.

Envoy:

How awful to have the ardent heart
    Of a manly man
    And the useless body of a weak woman.

19

BABA BUN'EI

Chōshū's Attack on the Imperial Palace

August 20, 1864

In the early 1860s, Kyoto became a hotbed of pro-imperial, anti-foreign activists, many from the Chōshū, Tosa, Mito, and Satsuma domains. A special Tokugawa militia, the Shinsengumi, succeeded in expelling these "loyalists" from Kyoto in the summer of 1864, but under the leadership of Kusaka Genzui, a student of Yoshida Shōin (Document 10) and Maki Izumi (Document 11), a group of men from Chōshū immediately plotted to retake the city. On August 20, 1864, some three thousand men armed with rifles and cannon tried to enter the gates of the imperial palace with the quixotic goal of restoring the emperor to direct rule. They were met and defeated by the forces of Aizu, Satsuma, and the Shinsengumi. Civil war replaced the tactics of terror; Kusaka, Maki, and four hundred other "loyalists" died, and battle fires in the center of the imperial city destroyed some 300,000 dwellings (Document 20). Once Kyoto was restored to Tokugawa control, Chōshū was officially declared an "enemy of the court."

Genji Yume Monogatari provides a unique documentary account of this major turning point in the restoration drama. It was compiled by Baba Bun'ei, a kimono dealer from Fukuoka resident in Kyoto and a collector of sensitive information with close ties to pro-imperial forces. His eyewitness account was published immediately after the battle and later, in 1905, translated into English by Ernest Satow, a British diplomat with experience in Japan.

The date was August 20, 1864. Before the day had dawned, and while the eastern sky was still dark, a loud roar arose suddenly, the report of cannon echoed repeatedly, and the steps of men and horses were faintly heard, though at a great distance. . . . As the noise of swift foot-steps became louder and louder, I was frightened by voices crying,

Baba Bun'ei, *Japan, 1853–1864; or, Genji Yume Monogatari*, trans. Ernest Mason Satow (Tokyo: Naigai Shuppan Kyōkai, 1905), 166–70, 171–72, 225, 226–27, 228, 236–39. Translation modified by the editors.

"See the lord of Chōshū marching forth." "This is dreadful," I thought, and rushed to open the door in my night attire. It was then I saw that Nakadachiuri street was full of spectators. Over their heads appeared banners and streamers, distinctly emblazoned with "Kunishi Shinano Tomosuke of Chōshū" in bright letters and with the crest of the Mōri family. I thought to myself, "Ah! Some great misfortune has happened," and tried to get nearer to see the procession. There was no mistake about it; it was the Chōshū officer Kunishi Shinano, from Tenryūji temple at Saga, with his whole force of more than three hundred men; their bodies were covered in armor, and they were advancing from the west up Nakadachiuri street, marshaled in companies and subdivisions, toward the Sacred Precincts of the Imperial Palace. The leader Shinano was clad in a suit of armor tied with grass-green silken strings, covered with an undergarment of Yamato brocade and over this he wore a surcoat of white gauze. . . . Before him went flags and banners and two field-pieces, with a company of thirty spearmen. Companies of forty or fifty musketeers preceded and followed him, in close array, marching towards the Nakadachiuri Gate of the Palace.

At that moment the gate was in the charge of Kuroda, the Prince of Chikuzen. His men guarded it vigilantly, closing the doors, and waited, swallowing their spittle, expecting an attack from this quarter. Fearing what might happen, I followed the rear of Chōshū force as far as the Muromachi street, and there saw the Hitotsubashi Regiment of musketeers coming up in close array from the south end of the street. I thought something would happen, but the Chōshū men quickly closed up to the north side of Nakadachiuri street, and left half the road vacant. The Hitotsubashi troops passed along the south side, brushing the flanks of the Chōshū men, right up to the front of the Nakadachiuri Gate, where they ensconced themselves behind bamboo shields. Spreading out their line they poured a continuous fire of musketry on the Chōshū force. . . .

For a moment the Chōshū force had begun to fall into disorder, but they closed their ranks again and dashed vigorously right at the center of the Hitotsubashi line, which, seeing the enemy advance to close quarters, broke and fled. The Chōshū men followed them up hotly, cutting them down on all sides. Some threw away their muskets and they began to flee southwards down Karasumaru street. The Chōshū men, who were determined not to let them escape, kept firing on them and they fled in all directions, without taking a stand.

At this moment the Hamaguri Gate division seemed to be in the thick of a hot engagement, and the discharge of firearms made a tremendous din. Abandoning the Nakadachiuri Gate, Kunishi's men pressed up to the Hamaguri Gate, driving the Hitotsubashi division before them. This gate was defended by the Aizu men, who were determined to die before they would suffer it to be taken.... [But the Chōshū force] broke through the Aizu line, and entered the Palace enclosure without difficulty, where a bloody fight ensued.

Just then the Chōshū men perceived Nomura Kangohei and Uchida Nakanosuke, two scouts from Satsuma, riding up Karasumaru street from the south, and taking them for enemies, fired on them. The latter drew their swords with a shout of defiance, and cut right into the middle of their assailants, without wavering in the least. Uchida cut his way through without much difficulty and retreated to the north, but being surrounded by a multitude Nomura was unable to escape and was killed. His head was cut off and placed on the top of a curbstone close in front of the Hamaguri Gate.

At this point a body of two hundred Satsuma men . . . came at the double quick from the northern end of Karasumaru street. Kunishi's rear was still at the corner of Karasumaru street, at Nakadachiuri, and did not know how the fight had gone in the front. When the Satsuma troops came down upon them and fired their muskets right and left at them, they turned around to meet the attack. The assistant strategist Katsura Kogorō[1] and Sakuma Konosuke, shouted to their men, "The enemy has appeared at our rear, look out," and forming the line the other way, ordered them to fire a volley. The Hitotsubashi force, which had just fled in disorder, took advantage of this movement to come to life again, and the Chōshū men now found themselves attacked at front and rear. Their spirits aroused, they fired their weapons, the hand-to-hand musketry combat lasting a considerable while. Both sides fired till the bullets fell as thick as raindrops, and the spears crossing each other looked like a hedge of bamboo-grass. . . .

I managed to find my way back to my own humble cottage. I sent my wife and children a long way off, for it was dangerous to leave them where they were, and I was preparing to flee also with a collection of our most precious belongings, when the roar of guns became more frequent and louder than ever. . . . When I went into the street, I found people of all classes, ages, and of both sexes in a fearful state of fright.

[1]Katsura later changed his name to Kido Takayoshi (1833–1877) and became an important figure in the early Meiji government. See Document 34.

They were carrying off their various possessions and running wildly to all points of the compass. The soldiery too, brandishing swords and spears, rushed hither and thither. Here and there were samurai fighting desperately, and the bullets flew overhead like pelting rain. There were helmets and pieces of armor that had been cast away by their owners, spears, pikes, bows, muskets and military equipment of all kinds lying about in quantities. Some of the townspeople had fled, throwing down their things in the street. Lying prostrate here and there were men who had fallen down wounded, and the roads were full of headless corpses. It was a sight that revolted the eyes. Steeling myself to these things, I got through them, and with great difficulty at last escaped from the town. . . .

Maki Izumi and Matsuyama Shinzō, with others . . . , had been the ringleaders in fanning the zeal of the Chōshū forces and of the low class samurai, and in inducing them to march on Kyoto and violate the sanctity of the imperial palace. How could they calmly sit down under defeat; with what face could they return home and meet everyone's eyes? Let the rest return to their country, and strive with all their might to do their duty loyally, but as for themselves they would die where they were, and let their deaths justify them. . . .

A cloud of black smoke rose to the heavens [from the top of Mount Tennō], apparently from some huts that had been set on fire. Judging from this that the enemy must have retreated, [Aizu forces] carefully formed a line and marched up to the top. On looking round they saw in the ashes of the huts the bodies of sixteen or seventeen men who had disemboweled themselves on a common bed of death. . . .

By the side of one of the bodies thus lying half scorched by fire was found a slip of paper containing Maki Izumi's farewell to the world. It ran as follows: "My patriotic soul, which has lived years and months, is buried among the stones on the great mountain's peak." . . .

Meanwhile, ferocious and excited soldiery fired cannon against the plaster storehouses still left standing, hoping to catch any fugitives who might have taken refuge in them. This was done without any warning and upon the slightest suspicion. . . . The fire gradually became more violent until the whole of the capital was wrapped in flames. From Ichijō street on the north the fire passed over Nijō and Sanjō to Shijō and Gojō. Ayano-kōji and Nishiki-no-kōji were also included in the general disaster. Rokkakudō was reduced to ashes, and even the enormous Bukkoji temple, with Rokujo and the temporary buildings of the eastern Honganji, disappeared in smoke in the twinkling of an eye. All the Shinto shrines and Buddhist temples, the residences of the nobles of the Court, the barracks of the daimyo, and the dwellings of the common people were involved without exception in one common conflagration. Even the grass on the fields was consumed by the flames.

This capital . . . entirely disappeared in one morning in the smoke of the flames of a war-fire, which was assisted in the work of destruction by a violent wind. Nothing was left of it but a burnt and scorched desert. Alas! . . .

On ordinary occasions, when a fire takes place, friends and relations hurry to the spot to help in carrying the property out of the burning houses. But on the present occasion no one went to the assistance of another; everyone was obliged to flee with his property and furniture burning before his eyes. Those who had friends in the neighboring villages went there in the hope of finding refuge, and supremely fortunate were those who were able to find shelter. For five or six days no commerce went on at all. . . . Even people with plenty of gold and silver died of hunger and exhaustion. Some went into the fields and stole eggplants and melons that they might eat but were killed by peasants. Warriors in armor broke into the few houses that had escaped burning, in broad daylight, without fear or shame. Brandishing their swords in a threatening manner, they seized gold and silver and clothing. There were many cases of this kind. That night no one had a roof to cover him and spent the night in the fields. As it was toward the end of summer and still terribly hot, the mosquitoes raised a shout and came on in hordes, till the poor wretches fancied that the enemy had come to attack them. The cries of the townspeople were heard loud and far, even above the hum of the mosquitoes. The sky was lit up by the flames as if it were broad daylight, and the roar of the cannon never ceased. . . . Palaces of the great and dwellings of the common people came tumbling down with a sound of general ruin, like the falling of hundreds and thousands of thunderbolts. Heaven and earth trembled and quaked, until the end of the world seemed to be at hand.

20

Kyoto: The Fires of War
August 20, 1864

Broadsheets quickly spread news of Chōshū's attack on the Tokugawa-allied forces guarding the imperial palace. Since most of the readers would have been commoners and it was the commoner wards that burned, it is perhaps not surprising that the broadsheet shown here highlights the collateral damage caused by the fires (the shaded area) in Kyoto.

To the right of the tongue of burned-out city blocks stretching to the north lies the imperial palace, with its outer ring of aristocratic compounds. They border on Karasumaru Street, and the two gates attacked by the Chōshū force, Nakadachiuri and Hamaguri, are located there. One block over is Muromachi Street. Just below where the area covered by the fire is more expansive, to the left or west side, lies Nijō Palace, home to the shoguns on their rare visits to the city. It, too, escaped damage. Maruta Street runs east and west above Nijō Palace; Nijō Street runs to it; Sanjō is the third large street that runs below it. Just east of the burned area on the south side of Sanjō is the Chōshū domain office. South of Nijō Palace can be found commoner wards that did not burn; Bukkōji and Rokakudō, which did, lie to the east. Mount Tennō, where Maki Izumi (Document 11) committed suicide, lies seven kilometers to the southwest of the map.

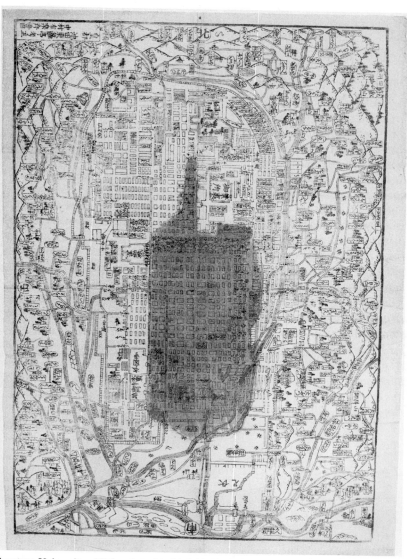

Courtesy University of Tokyo Interfaculty Initiative in Information Studies / Graduate School of Interdisciplinary Information Studies (Ono Hideo Collection).

21

Satirical Song on Current Events

1865

Following the attack by Chōshū forces on Kyoto, the shogunate dispatched an expeditionary force to punish the domain for its anti-Tokugawa and anti-Western activities. By the end of 1864, Tokugawa officials declared that Chōshū had submitted to shogunal authority, but this optimism proved illusory. Early in 1865, Takasugi Shinsaku, one of Yoshida Shōin's students (Document 10), organized an army of peasants and carried out a coup in Chōshū to restore power to pro-imperial forces. Shortly after the era name was changed from Genji (Original Rule) to Keiō (Jubilant Response) on May 1, 1865, the shogunate announced its intention to dispatch a second expeditionary force against Chōshū. This time, however, there was little enthusiasm for a fight. As a satirical poem put it, "The era name is changed to Keiō and we are ordered to advance, but read from below, this means to stop now!"[1]

Suspicious of any attempt to bolster shogunal power, Tokugawa allies refused to take part in the second expedition. Moreover, the shogun's army stationed in Osaka was unpopular with the local people, who blamed it for rising rice prices. They expressed their distrust of the shogunate and its officials in satirical poems, popular songs (like the one reproduced here), graffiti, and inflammatory posters. These sources provide a humorous critique of current events. As one inflammatory poster put it, "Good Government, All Sold Out!"

---

[1]The characters for Keiō in phonic script are read as *kei-oo*. "Read from below"—that is, read from the bottom up, since Japanese is written vertically—it becomes *oo-kei* or *oke*! This means to stop in one's tracks. "Read from below" can also mean "from the viewpoint of us commoners."

Yajima Takanori, ed., *Edo jidai rakusho ruijū*, vol. 3 (Tokyo: Tōkyōdō Shuppan, 1985), 120. Translated by M. William Steele.

A Counting Song

ONE (*hitotsu*): Men (*hito*) didn't want the trade that Ii Naosuke started, so now he's lost his head. Isn't that great!

TWO (*futatsu*): Deep (*fu*kai) plans there seemed to be, but they have yet to expel the barbarians. The samurai are such weaklings!

THREE (*mitsu*): Looking (*mi*te) strong in their war gear, they can't seem to get anywhere. What a farce!

FOUR (*yotsu*): Surely (*yo*moya) they don't dare go west, so why have they come this far? What cowards they are!

FIVE (*itsutsu*): Arrogant (*i*sei) samurai hold themselves in high regard, but weren't the shogun's bannermen defeated by the foreigners? They don't deserve their stipends!

SIX (*mutsu*): All (*mu*yami) the rooms in town are taken over; they pester us continually with unreasonable demands. What a bunch of lousy beggars!

SEVEN (*nanatsu*): In any case (*na*ni) peace will come only by defeating the foreigners. Don't they know what's most important?

EIGHT (*yatsu*): Always (*ya*tarani) shouting out "Subdue Chōshū!" will simply result in divine punishment. Such blasphemy!

NINE (*kokonatsu*): This (*ko*nna) defies all understanding. Why should four copper coins be worth twelve? Why do prices rise? What fools the officials are!

TEN (*to*): Stupid (*to*roi) looking men beat on a drum, but once the war cry is sounded, they all run away. What asses they are!

22

Sketch of the July 10, 1866, Edo Riot

Beginning in 1865, the price of rice and other commodities in Edo and Osaka rose suddenly owing to poor harvests and the stockpiling of food and goods in preparation for the shogun's second campaign against Chōshū. The year 1866 marked a peak in popular protest. There were 35 incidents in cities and 105 in the countryside, a record number for the Edo period. Most occurred between July and October, during the conflict with Chōshū.

In June 1866, townspeople destroyed commercial houses in the Kobe area. Beginning on June 25, the rioting spread throughout Osaka when city workers and farmers in nearby rural areas demanded lower prices, the return of pawned items, cancellation of debts, and food rationing. On July 10, Edo fell under siege. That day, the crowd attacked forty pawnshops, rice shops, saké shops, and inns around the city's eastern entrance. The number of protesters swelled on succeeding days; angry townsmen, sometimes as many as three thousand, armed with fire hooks, bamboo poles, mallets, and mauls, destroyed property throughout the city. In addition to rice and silk merchants and others connected with foreign trade, the mob singled out rich merchants who refused to donate money or food for poor relief.

Few died in the riots, and to some extent the townspeople were able to rectify economic inequalities and remind the rich and powerful of their obligation to treat the poor with compassion.

The illustration reproduced here comes from a contemporary account.

Tokyo National Museum.

23

Outbursts of Popular Discontent
July 24–31, 1866

Like urban centers, rural villages, especially in economically advanced areas, were hard hit by sudden rises in commodity prices. Farmers on shogunal lands also protested a tax designed to help pay the costs of the expedition against Chōshū. On July 24, 1866, immediately after the rioting in Edo subsided, a large-scale uprising broke out northwest of Edo. Many farmers there had recently converted from grain to mulberry, hoping to take advantage of the lucrative but risky Yokohama silk trade. The uprising engulfed the entire province of Musashi. For a week, some 100,000 farmers were on the march, wrecking shops, warehouses, residences, and offices belonging to rich merchants and other members of the village elite. One group even contemplated marching on Yokohama to attack the foreign settlement there. The rural protesters did not envision a new social order. Instead, their demands for cheaper rice and relief for the poor harked back to an ideal order in which the rich and powerful treated those less fortunate with benevolence. Not only was such compassion not forthcoming, but the uprisings in Musashi and other parts of the country also aided the collapse of any semblance of social and political order.

The first document in this selection comes from an 1866 chronicle, compiled by the Hiratsuka family located northwest of Edo, that seeks to explain the origins of the uprising. The second is from a broadsheet that circulated news of the uprising. The third, from a farmer's narrative, shows what consequences await stingy merchants who refuse to give relief to the poor.

Hiratsuka Household Document

If one were to trace the origins of the mob wreckings of July 24, 1866, one must go back fourteen or fifteen years, to the time when the black ships from a foreign country came to Shimoda harbor in Izu province. . . . The captain aboard the black ship was Matthew C. Perry of

Patricia Sippel, "Popular Protest in Early Modern Japan: The Bushū Outburst," *Harvard Journal of Asiatic Studies* 37, no. 2 (December 1977): 273, 297–98; "Shinpan uchikowashi kudoki," 1866. Saitama Prefectural Museum of History and Folklore. Translated by M. William Steele.

Washington, the capital of the country of America. He petitioned repeatedly for trade and commerce. At the time the black ships arrived, Japanese ancestral law dictated that they should be driven away but, because of the long-continued peace, military defenses had become extremely weak. Revitalizing them was exceedingly difficult. Consequently, maintaining that to expel the foreigners would be impossible, the shogunate acceded to their request and granted their petition.

The shogunate made land available in a place called Yokohama, where it supplied foreign merchants with lodging-houses numbering more than two hundred. Japanese merchants built houses in the same area and sold various wares. Merchants called wholesalers both from our country and overseas joined in adorning themselves with elegance and pursuing profit. . . . Consequently, the cost of rice and other goods rose steadily, until this year (1866) prices reached great heights: 1 *ryō* [a large gold coin that usually bought approximately 10 *to* of rice] could buy only 1.1 *to* [one *to* equals approximately 18 liters] of white rice and 2.5 *to* of barley. Other goods were priced accordingly.

In these circumstances, common people were exceptionally impoverished. It was said that the world was truly riotous. No sooner had reports arrived of property destruction in Osaka and the area of Hyōgo [Kobe] than bouts of wrecking occurred along the Eastern Highway in the Kantō region including various sections of Edo. It indeed happened before our very eyes.

A Tale of Wrecking

Now, I'm going to tell you
A fine tale of uproar and riot.
It takes place in the Province of Musashi
And in the District of Chichibu.
In eighteen villages all within hearing distance of the bell of
The Ne-no-Gongen temple,
There lived a man of high repute.
He was from the large village of Naguri.
His name was Sugiyama Giyuemon.
He owned lands worth 800 *koku* [one *koku* equals 5.1 bushels of
    rice]
And had a fortune of 6,000 *ryō* [one *ryō* could buy 1 *koku* of rice] to
    boot.
But when the prices of things climbed so high
He took pity on all the needy people of his village.

He gave all his money for their relief.
And now all the villagers have felt it necessary
To meet together and discuss their problems.
They talked about the merchants from throughout the land
Who dealt in rice and other grains and
Traded with foreign countries, saying that
If they continued to profit in this way
The people will die from starvation.
The people decided to risk their lives,
Wreck the houses of all the wealthy,
And thereby try to get the prices of things to come down.
Sugiyama was made the leader of the march.
On a large banner was drawn a rice bowl and crossed rice paddles
Underneath was written "World Renewing God."
And with this flag in the lead
About 3,000 marched off on July 22, 1866.
All assembled armed with hoes, bamboo poles, and large saws.
Everyone tried to be at the front.
First they wrecked the rich of Akano.
And then moved on to Ome and Hanno and then on to Ogimachi
    and Kurosu.
Everywhere the houses of the rich were wrecked.

From a Farmer's Narrative

In Kawashima-Sonobe village there was a rich man known as Etchū-ten or Shirami. He had risen from extreme poverty. When he built his first storehouse he reflected that, since lice (*shirami*) are creatures which breed naturally, he would like to increase his money in a similar manner. So he printed on the shed the character *shirami*. On all the storehouses which he built subsequently he affixed the *shirami* character. His only hobby was to increase gold and silver in the manner of lice. Inexcusably, he hated to lend and, even more, he hated to give in charity. . . .

An urgent message came that the riot forces had already reached the next village. Immediately he thought of hiding his money, but he had no place to put it. Then, suddenly, he hit upon the idea of hiding it by stuffing it amongst the chaff in his woodshed.

Soon the rioters arrived, guided by the local headman. First, they announced: "You must contribute 3,000 *ryō* [of gold] and 300 *hyō* [of grain] to save the poor people of the area."

Since he was at heart a stingy man, he had the headman negotiate for a 2,000 *ryō* and 200 *hyō* donation. And so time passed. Meanwhile, people from various villages had assembled.

"Since he is at heart a stingy and uncompassionate man, we cannot have dealings with him, even if our lives depend on it. We must quickly destroy his property. . . ."

Forming two teams, the rioters tore down the house. Not confining themselves to small household effects, they destroyed everything, from the dwelling itself to storehouses, storerooms, sheds, woodsheds, stables, etc. All were smashed to pieces. [The rioters] threw pawned goods into the river and wells. They tore open bundles of grain and, mixing the five grains, piled them in a heap like a mountain. Stepping into it, they could hardly move. They broke the hoops on barrels of saké, soy sauce, and paraffin oil and the conflux was like a river. They pulled the lids off several tens of bean-paste barrels and there were some who called: "Mix chaff with it!"

So they looked for the woodshed and as they were about to rake out the chaff they discovered something else: the money that had been hidden previously. It was said that the boxes of thousand-*ryō* coins were piled as high as a mountain. As they raked them out, they saw all sorts of old coins. . . . Smashing open the boxes, the rioters said:

"The people of the village should come and collect these."

They scattered the gold and silver as a storm scatters snow in the garden. Indeed, the savings which, through lack of compassion [the "lice" merchant] had accumulated over many years were reduced at once to nothing. . . . On the following day, children from all around came and picked up the gold as they would pick up shells by the seashore.

5

Meiji Restoration

24

FUKUZAWA YUKICHI

Memorial Proposing a Shogunal Monarchy

September 7, 1866

Fukuzawa Yukichi (1835–1901) was Japan's leading westernizer in the years following the Meiji Restoration. The opening words of his book An Encouragement of Learning, *published in serial form starting in 1872, championed equality: "Heaven does not create one man above or below another man." In the early 1860s, his expertise in Dutch and English allowed him to accompany shogunal diplomatic missions to the United States and Europe as a translator. In 1866 he published his first major book,* Conditions in the West, *and in 1867 he opened a school of Western learning that would become Keiō University.*

Despite later protestations of neutrality, he was a strong supporter of the Tokugawa regime in the years preceding its collapse. His 1866 memorial, a written statement presented to the shogunate, advocated that the means be found to crush the Chōshū rebels and restructure Japan's government as a monarchy under the shogun's leadership. He saw the impending civil war in Japan in simple terms: The shogunate was on the side of order and progress, whereas Chōshū represented chaos and retrogression. This memorial shows the young Fukuzawa willing to use propaganda and military force to bring about Japan's standing as a civilized country.

M. William Steele, "Fukuzawa Yukichi and the Idea of a Shogunal Monarchy: Some Documents in Translation," special issue, *Asian Cultural Studies* 7 (March 1997): 20–23.

The deluded notion to "respect the emperor and expel the barbarians" (*sonnō-jōi*) has spread throughout the land since the time when treaties with foreign countries were first concluded. Due to this, great turmoil has arisen within the country. The court has been constantly troubled. In the end it would seem that the meaning of this slogan has nothing to do with respecting the emperor or with expelling the foreigners. Rather it is simply a tricky pretext to give wandering vagrants a chance to seek sustenance and further a chance for various daimyo who hold sinister designs to deviate further and further from the instructions of the Tokugawa family. . . . Chōshū is the number one rebel among the various daimyo and has begun mutinous plots. Therefore the plans now to attack and punish Chōshū are most welcome. Thanks to this one event we can expect that the Tokugawa family will be brought closer to the day of its revitalization.

. . . I pray that now we should resolutely decide to subjugate Chōshū in one fell swoop and with this momentum go on to reassert control over the various daimyo and [the court in] Kyoto, so that the shogun's government will be able to conduct international relations without interference. . . .

Point 1: Block avenues of communication between the Chōshū rebels and the foreign powers! Announce the charges against Chōshū to the world!

As already noted regarding the true intentions of the Chōshū rebels, the *sonnō-jōi* they advocate has been, right from the outset, only a pretext. Two years ago, after their defeat at Shimonoseki, Chōshū men repeatedly approached foreigners [for assistance]. They endeavored to send students overseas; they invited dishonest merchants to Shimonoseki and other places to carry on secret trade; and they purchased much weaponry. . . . Since at this time Chōshū has determined to make ready for the inevitable, it is all the more necessary to devise a policy, poor though it may be, for us [the shogunate] to purchase weapons from the foreigners, to borrow money, and if it comes to the worst, to depend upon the vagrant foreigners by employing foreign warships. Since this is treading the same path as the Chinese in suppressing the Taiping rebels [defeated in 1864], it is difficult to forecast the eventual outcome. Necessarily, this decision must be considered carefully. . . .

We have already sent a fourteen-point statement of the charges against Chōshū to the consul of each country. However, as mentioned above, Chōshū has dispatched students overseas to campaign on its behalf. They naturally aim only at Chōshū's advantage, proclaiming far-fetched opinions, and of course slandering the position of the shogunate. There is one faction that advocates a daimyo confederation, an idea currently discussed in newspapers.[1] Critical of the present government's management of affairs, this argument holds that the existing treaties with foreign nations should be annulled and that the various daimyo should form a union much like the German confederation. The various daimyo of this new confederation should then individually conclude treaties. It seems that the British envoy [Harry] Parkes and others are secretly in agreement with this proposal. Furthermore, Satsuma and other domains are sending students overseas and all of them support this sort of daimyo confederation. Naturally, the overseas students discuss matters with the Chōshū students and believe what they say. If these students go about preaching and writing in newspapers in favor of a daimyo confederation, they may temporarily influence public opinion, and I daresay that they might change the course of deliberations now underway between Japan and several foreign countries. If by chance, something like this should happen, needless to say, a civil war will break out and all of Japan and the fortunes of the Tokugawa family will be in turmoil, resulting in irrevocable harm far greater than Chōshū's present treason. We must do something immediately in order to prevent this from happening.

. . . At this time a resident minister should be dispatched to the capital city of each nation. It is a general custom among nations that have concluded treaties to conduct diplomatic business by mutually exchanging ambassadors. However, we have so far postponed this obligation. . . .

If we send resident ministers to every country, diplomacy will become in all ways thorough and efficient and our intentions all the more clear. . . . Moreover, it is imperative to have a newspaper announcement about the dispatch of resident ministers, and proclaim our nation's justification of its views, including, of course, a refutation of the daimyo confederation argument. Turning the tables on the Chōshū rebels, we should announce one by one, even the most trivial, the charges, old and new, against them. Issue this every day and finally the world will detest the sins of Chōshū, and it will come to be said that those who are friendly with Chōshū know neither honor nor dignity. . . .

---

[1]This is probably a reference to the series by Ernest Satow titled "English Policy" published in the *Japan Times* in December 1865 and 1866, which described the real rulers of Japan as the daimyo, not the shogun nor the emperor. Translated into Japanese, it exerted great influence on political thinking in 1866.

Point 2: Suppression of civil war by use of foreign aid

For the past two years Chōshū has been secretly making military preparations to defend itself against the impending punitive expedition. It has westernized both its weaponry and its military tactics. Furthermore, the people of the domain are passionately hostile to the shogunate. Therefore they are not an insignificant enemy. . . .

. . . At present, with the strength each side possesses, I am deeply worried over the outcome of the war. Such being the case, we should decide to call on the help of the military power of foreign countries and thereby with one fell swoop smash the two provinces of Nagato and Suo [which make up Chōshū]. Of course we must take into consideration the fact that relying upon foreign military power may cause popular unrest and that the expenses incurred will be enormous. This argument may be true in times of peace. . . . Now, however, with the impending fear that suddenly Japan may be involved in a civil war, and considering the fact that popular unrest is already at its zenith, the above consideration should be dropped. No longer is public sentiment swayed by the various ideas of the world — only military power can bring the nation under control. . . . Therefore, now at a time when the Chōshū rebels are opposing government forces in actual battle, if by some chance they should win, they would then change their name from "enemy of the court" to "supporter of the court" and graciously give to the shogun the name "enemy of the court." Such being the case, correct naming depends entirely upon the strength and weakness of military power. Such things as imperial proclamations, similar to the edicts of the pope in Rome, are merely embellishments to military power. . . .

Accordingly it should be resolved without hesitation to crush the two provinces of Nagato and Suo with the help of foreign military power, and furthermore to direct the banner of subjugation directly against the various daimyo who opposed the views of the shogunate. With this one action I think that [the shogunate] should be able to exhibit its power to the extent that it completely transforms the feudal system throughout all of Japan.

25

SAKAMOTO RYŌMA

The Domain Question

December 1867

*Sakamoto Ryōma (1836–1867) is celebrated as one of the heroes of
the Meiji Restoration. Like hundreds of other "men of high purpose,"
he was impatient with established authority. Trained as a swordsman,
he believed that direct action against both the shogunate and foreigners
was required. He changed his mind when he encountered Katsu Kaishū
(author of Document 29) in 1862. To open the country was to strengthen
the country. Katsu's critique of the Tokugawa order, his plan for national
unity, and his vision of Japan's future national power and greatness
made sense to the young patriot from Tosa, but he never fully supported
the shogunate. Although Ryōma worked with Katsu to create a national
navy, after Katsu's progressive views came under attack by Tokugawa
hard-liners in 1866, Ryōma helped to negotiate an alliance between
Satsuma and Chōshū. In 1867 he mediated the shogun's voluntary return
of governing authority to the emperor (Document 28). Ryōma was assassinated shortly thereafter, but he played a decisive role in bringing about
the Meiji Restoration.*

*The following selection reflects Ryōma's thinking at this important
turning point. For him, Japan's revolution depended on respect for popular opinion and the adoption of democratic methods of decision making,
beginning at the domain level. The document itself is incomplete, inter-
rupted perhaps by his death.*

Part I: Treating of the Revolution Generally

Few are they who, appreciating the spirit of the age, can foresee that a
movement will succeed or fail. . . . Possessing in a preeminent degree
this rare statesmanlike sagacity, two men have achieved for themselves
a name that the subsequent events vindicated. One, in ancient times,

Chikami Kiyoomi, *Sakamoto Ryōma* (Tokyo: Hakubunkan, 1914), 249–63. Translation
modified by the editors.

was Masashige,[1] who, perceiving that in his generation the government of the country by the emperor was no longer possible, died by his own hand in Minatogawa; soon after, the executive power fell into the hands of the military houses. The other, in modern times, is the Shogun [Tokugawa Yoshinobu], who, foreseeing the impossibility of his retaining the reins of power any longer, resigned of his own accord; immediately after, the authority of the emperor, with all its prerogatives restored, was established in one symmetrically organized administrative structure. Now, if the good government of the Empire is to be secured thereby, it is just and right that the control should be vested even in the people; if the affairs of the nation are thrown into confusion, it is unjust and wrong, though it be done by the highest Dignity [i.e. the emperor]. The principle is that the exercise of the national authority is subject to the approval or otherwise of public opinion. And the rule that applies to the government of the empire is surely not less applicable to the government of the domains.

The great majority of the daimyo are generally persons who have been born and nurtured in the seclusion of the women's apartments; who have been cherished as tenderly as if they were delicate ornaments of jewels or pearls; who, even when they have grown up to a man's estate, still exhibit all the traits of childhood; having never mastered the details of business, they feel no sense of responsibility in approaching the affairs of state. Leading a life of leisure, they succeed to the inheritance of their ancestors. With their bodies clad in gorgeous apparel, they feel not the winter's blast and know not that men pine of starvation and cold. With the beauty of their wives and concubines arrayed before them, and the sounds of music and revelry ringing in their ears, they leave no desire of the heart ungratified. Even now that the symptoms of their decline have unmistakably set in, they are intent only on the pleasures that yet remain to be exhausted. As wisely might they pray to the gods for perpetual youth, or seek from the fairies the boon of immortality. And in the same category are those who, though designated vassals, are born of good family on the great estates. Not only the lords but also the vassals are such as are here described. Hence the offices are constantly filled by unqualified men, and corruption is so rife as to defy all attempts to suppress it. How, pray, while things remain in this condition,

---

[1] Kusunoki Masashige (1294–1336) served as the unrivaled paragon of loyalty for having fought against impossible odds for the restoration of direct rule by the emperor following the fall of the Kamakura shogunate.

can any scheme for promoting the prosperity or power of the nation be concerted or carried out?

Part II: Unfolding the Basis on Which Reforms Should Be Initiated

On a cursory view of the organization and customs of the various domains, there is apparent—notwithstanding a general likeness in the main—an absence of uniformity in the arrangement of the official departments and in the relative numbers of the official body. There is, however, one usage, which without a single exception is observed in all the domains: Clear distinctions of social rank, high and low, are maintained. Political office and distribution of income are awarded accordingly.

In laying the foundation of reform in the administration of the domains, three measures that require immediate attention are as follows:

1. The head of the domain should first issue instructions to the retainers to the effect that the old customs are to be abolished and an entirely new system to be inaugurated; and in order to preclude diversity of opinion or change of purpose regarding this step, he should require the whole retainer band to enter into a special covenant and to ratify it by going through the ceremony of an oath. . . .

2. Having first bound the retainers by a sworn covenant in this manner, the head of the domain should next do away with the observance of distinctions of family, put an end to the custom of hereditary incomes, and dismiss at one stroke the entire body of officers regardless of all degrees of precedence, thus blending the whole band together and reducing them to a common level so as to constitute an entirely homogeneous community, similar to an ordinary public assemblage. This effected, the next step should be to fix beforehand on a certain definite number of vacancies in proportion to the size of the domain and the number of vassals and to let each one put forward the individual of his choice; that is to say, by means of the vulgar institution of the ballot, there should be an election made of the distinguished men who command the majority of supporters. . . .

3. When this operation of public election has been once gone through, the eligible candidates will be thereby discriminated from those who are ineligible. This done, the head of the domain should then take this batch, who have been drafted in the

preliminary poll, and, having once more prescribed the number required, should instruct them to return, by a second and decisive election, their ablest men; the residue of gentlemen who fail to be elected should be told to wait further orders.

The practice of selecting gifted men by popular suffrage prevails widely in all the enlightened countries of the West; but there, being an institution of long-standing, it is familiar even to children. Yet our own domains have not yet heard of the existence of this custom. Hence, although it is an eminently ingenious device, there are always sure to be dolts within a domain. Although it is an essentially enlightened custom, a domain is never altogether wanting in clodhoppers, and for an intelligent man to explain the device to blockheads, or for an enlightened chief to work out the custom with senseless retainers, is just about as much use as asking a blind man whether he prefers a subdued tint or a bright one or consulting a deaf man as to whether a note should be sharp or flat. Thus it is that the common mass generally never thoroughly comprehend the matter; and when at times they do receive orders to hold an election, either they vote according to their own personal liking or grudges, without either looking for qualifications or objecting to the want of them; or they choose from among their immediate acquaintances, according to the strength of their intimacy, neither singling out men of talent, nor sifting out the incapables; or again, they support an influential man through fear of his power or, it may be, reject a humble man from dislike of his low rank, thus acting the part of the child in the vulgar adage who doesn't know its parent's mind. From this it follows that simply to appoint those who had the most votes in a single polling would not necessarily be to secure the most suitable men. This is the reason for the provision that a second poll must be taken; and in committing to the candidates returned in the first instance, instead of to the whole domain, the duty of making the second and final election — still adhering to the original principle of the highest number of votes — the idea, of course, is that any blunders committed in the preparatory selection will be eliminated in the repetition of the process.

26

Ee ja nai ka
1867

Following an abundant harvest in 1867, strange things started happening. Talismans bearing the names of gods and Buddhas seemingly fell from the sky. Taking them to be signs that a new, bountiful world had come, commoners danced in the streets and chanted "Ee ja nai ka"—"Ain't it great" or "What the hell." Men dressed as women, women as men, paraded through town and village, going from house to house and accepting offerings of food and drink. In total disregard of social convention, they shouted obscenities at the top of their voices. Although historians have documented where the dances broke out and when, they are at a loss to explain why. Was it a plot by Chōshū activists accused of dropping the first talismans? Was it a form of religious hysteria? Was it a way to relieve stress in a time of political uncertainty?

Each region made up its own chants. Some gave thanks for world renewal, as in "This year the world is being renewed; ain't it great," or "Let's dance for a bountiful year; how auspicious." Others proclaimed sexual liberation, shouting, "Anything goes!" Still others contained a political message: "With Chōshū's coming, prices have fallen; ain't it great." Something of the movement's complexity is evident in the following selections and in Document 27.

Four "Ee Ja Nai Ka" Chants

Butterflies [a reference to Chōshū] have flown in from the west,
Seeking money at Kobe's shores,
Ee ja nai ka, ee ja nai ka! Ain't that great.

People who worship the gods sincerely
Will bequeath good fortune to their descendants.

Kyōdo kenkyū 4, no. 7 (October 1917): 438; Nishitake Seiji, *Ee ja nai ka: minshū undō no keifū* (Tokyo: Shinbunsha Ōraisha, 1973), 273–74; and Yamaguchi Yoshikazu, *Awaji ee ja nai ka* (Tokushima: Tokushima Dozoku Geijutsu Kenkyūjo, 1931), 95–98, all translated by M. William Steele; Satow Diary, December 13 and 15, 1867, Ernest Satow Papers, Japan, 33/15–17, Public Record Office, London; Rebecca L. Copeland, *The Sound of the Wind: The Life and Works of Uno Chiyo* (Honolulu: University of Hawai'i Press, 1992), 132–33.

Isn't that right!
Boisterous pilgrims have begun to give thanks
Soon the day of true purification will be upon us.
Isn't that right!
What a dreadful year it was [1866]. Let's forget it!
Thanks to the gods we can dance. Isn't that right!

Japan is going to be renewed. Isn't that great!
Let's celebrate the abundant harvest by dancing.
Let's set off on a pilgrimage.
Isn't that great!

The gods will descend upon the country of Japan,
But rocks will rain on the residences of the foreigners.
Ee ja nai ka, ee ja nai ka! Ain't that great!

From the Diary of Ernest Satow, Interpreter for the British Legation

Dec. 13, Fri. There were 7 days of feasting in Kobe in honor of the expected opening of the port and processions of red crepe dressed people with carts, supposed to convey earth for the filling up of the settlement site. Fêtes also to be in Hyōgo site of settlement. . . . [After returning to Osaka] Walked at a great rate through crowds of festival makers, dancing and singing *i ja nai ka, i ja nai ka, i ja nai-i ka*. Houses decorated with cakes in all colors, oranges, little bags and straw and flowers. Dresses chiefly red crepe also blue and purple. Many people carrying red lanterns on their heads, and dancing. The whole in honor of the shower of pieces of paper bearing the names of the two gods of Ise, which has lately taken place.

Dec. 15, Sun. We found some difficulty in forcing our way through the crowds of merrymakers dressed in red flaming garments and shouting *i ja nai ka*, isn't it nice. They were so occupied with their dancing and their lanterns that we were quite unnoticed and I was afraid that the escort would provoke a quarrel by the violent manner in which they thrust the people aside to let us pass. On the contrary however they made way for us without offering the slightest rudeness. Arrived at Tokaku [but] we found the chief rooms occupied by festival makers and the rest of the place shut up. . . . Whilst we stood there trying to persuade them to give us a room, a herd of young boys & men trooped in shouting and dancing

[who] tossed about in their midst a *kago* [palanquin] with a fat doll most gorgeously dressed. All the feasters in the house came to meet them on the thresholds of the various entrances, and after a violent dance on both sides in concert, the troop disappeared again.

The Recollections of an Old Man in the 1920s

Everyone was up and celebrating the changes taking place. Men and women, grandpas and grandmas . . . didn't matter who . . . everyone was up and shouting "Well, why not! Anything goes!" They'd burst into a stranger's house shouting and carrying on—didn't much care if the owner cursed them or laughed at them. Some of the merrymakers hid their faces behind masks and some painted theirs up, but others just went with the face they were born with. They'd eat all the rice cakes they could lay their hands on, and they'd drink their fill of liquor, too. But as soon as they'd be full, why someone'd shout "Let's dance a bit till we're hungry again!" and they'd all set in to dancing. "Well, why not! Anything goes!"

A group of fellows set out like that, dressed only in their loincloths. Didn't have a penny to their name, but they made it all the way to Ise Shrine feasting and dancing. I wasn't but a little fellow at the time so I could only follow after them as far as the neighboring village. Oh my, it was some celebration—the likes of which I've never seen. Yes, I'd have to say that was the most interesting moment in my life.

The next-door neighbors'd be at their spring cleaning—when along would come a gust of wind and carry off their prized paper charm. It'd land down the road a ways, and then someone'd come along and pick it up. The next thing you know, he'd be carrying on like it was a blessing from heaven. Yes indeed, thought that charms had just fallen out of the sky! Why even when folks came across an old Daikoku [god of wealth] charm lying in the road, they'd set into dancing, shouting all the while, "Look! Oh look! A blessing from Heaven!" Happened so often the little dance they did came to be known as the "blessing from Heaven Jig." Oh, I suppose a blessing from heaven was reason enough to celebrate because soon the whole household'd be up and dancing. "Well, why not! Anything goes!" they'd holler, and they'd dance on down to their neighbor's house, shouting and carrying on. And when they were done there, they'd march right on to the next house. "Well, why not! Anything goes!" It got to be that for a whole half a year or so no one could do a lick of work. And then the Fushimi Battle [on January 27, 1868] put an end to it all.

27

Scroll Depicting the Ee Ja Nai Ka *Dancers*
November 1867

The ee ja nai ka *craze began in the summer of 1867 and quickly spread up and down the east coast of Japan. The first report of religious amulets and miniature images falling out of the skies came on August 13 from villages southeast of Nagoya. The dancing frenzy then spread from Nagoya to Kyoto, and reached Osaka in November. By the end of the year commoners as far south as Hiroshima were dancing. To the north, the movement spread to the Yokohama area in mid-November.*

The carnival atmosphere that prevailed in Fujisawa, a post station on the Tōkaidō (Eastern Coast Highway) just south of Yokohama, was recorded in a scroll written and illustrated by a village headman and his son who witnessed the event. Titled "On the Descent of Images of Buddhist and Shinto Deities," the initial scenes focus on the festivities; the final panels are more political. One shows villagers in mourning attire carrying a coffin; in fact, they are putting the Tokugawa shogunate to rest. The flag they display refers to the founder of the Tokugawa regime, Tokugawa Ieyasu, calling him by his posthumous name, "Eastern Shining Deity at Mount Nikkō." One wonders if the news of Yoshinobu's surrender of political authority to the emperor (Document 28) had already reached the ears of the revelers. Another scene shows local people giving vent to xenophobic feelings by throwing stones at two foreigners on horseback.

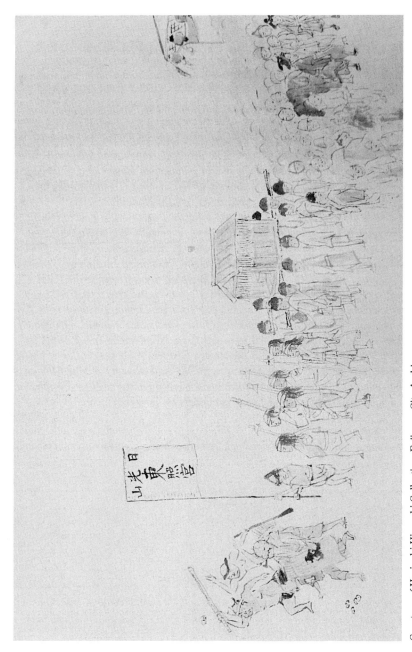

28

On the End of the Shogunate
November 1867–January 1868

In 1867 the war against Chōshū went badly, while rioting in Edo and the surrounding countryside further discredited the Tokugawa regime. The new shogun, Yoshinobu, attempted self-strengthening programs, but his plans backfired, causing even former supporters to call for his resignation. In March, Sakamoto Ryōma (Document 25) mediated an alliance between Chōshū and Satsuma directed against the shogunate. On October 29, the former lord of Tosa, Yamauchi Toyoshige, sent a memorial to Yoshinobu asking him to return his governing authority to the emperor and establish a deliberative council in Kyoto. Aware that Satsuma and Chōshū were plotting to overthrow him, Yoshinobu followed his advice. On November 9, he formally requested that administrative authority be returned to the court. Later, on November 19, he relinquished the title of shogun, for reasons given in the first selection here, thereby marking the end not only of the Tokugawa regime but also of the military governments that had characterized Japan since the establishment of the Kamakura shogunate in 1192.

Afraid that Yoshinobu would seek to regain power as the emperor's closest adviser, Satsuma and Chōshū determined that military action was necessary. On January 3, 1868, troops from Satsuma and other anti-Tokugawa domains seized the palace gates. An edict restoring imperial rule was issued; the office of the shogun and offices through which the shogunate controlled the court were abolished. Enomoto Takeaki, a Tokugawa retainer in Kyoto, sent Katsu Kaishū a letter describing the coup d'état and the atmosphere in Kyoto at the time. That letter also is excerpted here.

Meiji Japan through Contemporary Sources, vol. 2, *1844–1882* (Tokyo: Centre for East Asian Cultural Studies, 1970), 64–65; Katsube Mitake, Matsumoto Sannosuke, and Ōguchi Yūjirō, eds., *Katsu Kaishū Zenshū*, vol. 18 (Tokyo: Keisō Shobō, 1972), 445–47, translated by M. William Steele.

Tokugawa Yoshinobu's Letter of Resignation, November 19, 1867

A retrospect of the various changes through which the empire has passed shows us that after the decadence of the monarchical authority, power passed into the hands of the ministers of state; and that, owing to the civil wars of the Hogen [1156–1159] and Heiji [1159–1160] periods, the administrative power fell into the hands of the military class. My ancestor received more confidence and favor from the Court than any of his predecessors, and his descendants have succeeded him for more than two hundred years. Though I fill the same office, almost all of the acts of the administration are far from perfect, and I confess it with shame that the present unsatisfactory condition of affairs is due to my shortcomings and incompetence. Now that foreign intercourse becomes daily more extensive, unless the government is directed from one central authority, the foundations of the state will fall to pieces. If, however, the old order of things be changed, and the administrative authority be restored to the Imperial Court, and if national deliberations be conducted on an extensive scale, and the imperial decision be secured, and if the empire be supported by the efforts of the whole people, then the empire will be able to maintain its rank and dignity among the nations of the earth. Although I have allowed all the feudal lords to state their views without reserve, yet it is, I believe, my highest duty to realize these ideals by giving up entirely my rule over this land.

Letter from Enomoto Takeaki to Katsu Kaishū, January 8, 1868

Before my eyes the nation's situation has deteriorated to such an extent that I sigh in grief. . . . As you may well know, the ideas of four domains [Tosa, Echizen, Satsuma, and Uwajima] and others sympathetic to the Tokugawa family went into the formulation of the Tosa memorial that was presented to the shogun at the end of October. In Kyoto and Osaka there were outbreaks of violence, assassinations, and much-heated argumentation; however, at that point Yoshinobu seemed to have thoughts of his own concerning the matter and [in November] presented a petition to restore political authority to the court. Thereafter Kyoto was peaceful for a while. Under imperial summons the daimyo began to assemble in Kyoto. There arose much debate over evidence that Satsuma was scheming rebellion. Chōshū, moreover, had taken advantage of the impending opening of Hyōgo and Osaka harbors. . . .

Then, on January 2, 1868, they all advanced on Kyoto, their number being about fifteen hundred.

An imperial order restored Chōshū's court rank and permitted its entry into Kyoto. On the night of the 3rd, a decree demanding the resignation of the shogun was issued. On the 4th, the office of Kyoto protector held by Aizu was abolished, as was the office of Kyoto deputy held by Kuwana. . . .

The nine gates of the palace were seized by Satsuma and Hiroshima domain troops bearing unsheathed swords, lances, and rifles; there is even some evidence that they are planning to advance on our headquarters at Nijō Castle. On the 4th and 5th the Tokugawa soldiers plus troops from Aizu, Kuwana, Todo, Hikone, Kii, and other domains gathered at Nijō Castle and waited out the night beside bonfires. It was clear that they were ready to go out and fight. The figures of young and old were seen nodding to each other as they ran through the city.

All the pro-Tokugawa lords have decided upon war, but Yoshinobu has not issued the order to fight. Nonetheless, all of Kyoto is like a battleground. The people are naturally uneasy. This is a most terrifying and perplexing event, especially for those who do not understand the logic of the situation. . . . The combined strength of the Tokugawa family and its allies is three times as great as that of Satsuma, Chōshū, Tosa, and Hiroshima, whose combined forces total but six thousand men. On the 5th there was a meeting at the imperial palace. It was clear that Tosa strongly opposed the use of force. Chōshū also seemed to have softened its position. Only Satsuma is scheming rebellion as before. Yoshinobu did not attend this court meeting in which the following matters were decided. These matters have not yet been made public. . . .

The offices of supreme councilor, senior councilor, and junior councilor have been established and the entire government of the nation is to be directed personally by the emperor. Prince Arisugawa has been appointed supreme councilor; Princes Ninnaiji and Yamashina, nobles Nakayama Tadayoshi, Sanjō Sanetomi, and Nakamikado Tsuneyuki, and daimyo Tokugawa Yoshikatsu (Owari), Matsudaira Keiei (Echizen), Asano Nagakoto (Hiroshima), Yamauchi Toyoshige (Tosa), and Shimazu Tadayoshi (Satsuma) have been appointed senior councilors. The junior councilors are to be the nobles Ohara Shigetomi, Madenokōji Hirofusa, Hase Nobutsu, Iwakura Tomomi, and Hashimoto Saneyasu, and three retainers each from the five domains [Owari, Echizen, Hiroshima, Tosa, and Satsuma]. As you can see, this distribution of offices is quite unjust. I have no idea how the Tokugawa family will respond. Only chaos can describe the present situation.

29

KATSU KAISHŪ

Argument against Civil War

January 17, 1868

On January 3, 1868, pro-imperial troops led by Satsuma took posses-
sion of the imperial palace in Kyoto and proclaimed the restoration of
imperial rule. Although the office of shogun was abolished, the fate of the
Tokugawa family remained unclear. Tokugawa officials debated whether
or not to initiate hostilities. In Edo, terrorist activities carried out by
Satsuma agitators served to heighten prowar sentiments. Katsu Kaishū
(1823–1899), a naval officer and advocate of parliamentary-style
reform, argued against war, saying that it would only deepen domestic
unrest and invite foreign intervention. No one was listening, and on Jan-
uary 17, ten days before the Battle of Toba-Fushimi that began Japan's
civil war, Katsu resigned his navel commission and dispatched an irate
letter to Yoshinobu, the deposed shogun and head of what remained of
the old regime. His letter well describes the chaos of the times, his fears of
national collapse, and also his hopes for the establishment of a democratic
style of government in the future.

In the future the general situation of the nation will not be determined
by family reputation or status, but necessarily by just and righteous principles; not by private selfish principles, but by open public principles. Of
this there can be no doubt whatsoever. The fact that such a system of
justice has not yet been implemented is due to the stupidity of the officials and their devotion to the evil custom of national seclusion. Recently
travel to foreign countries has become easier and even commoners are
able to move freely in all directions. For this reason, great changes have
taken place, with every day bringing new things; there can be no com-
parison with the past. The common people are daily becoming more
intelligent, whereas the upper classes are daily becoming more ignorant. This is what causes confusion in Edo. It is impossible to obtain
peace and stability owing to mistaken, evil laws.

Katsube Mitake, Matsumoto Sannosuke, and Ōguchi Yūjirō, eds., *Katsu Kaishū Zenshū*,
vol. 18 (Tokyo: Keisō Shobō, 1972), 448–51. Translated by M. William Steele.

Over these past five or six years, members of court and the shogun-ate have simply been making excuses, saying this and that. Everyone, from the daimyo down to the commoners, has been engaged in promoting wild ideas in Kyoto, Osaka, and Edo. In fact, however, they have no idea why government exists; instead, they try to determine national policy on an arbitrary basis. This is a mistake brought about by their adherence to hereditary status considerations. They do not understand what true national policy is, nor have they thought deeply about what government means. What is called true government keeps the entire nation in peace and cares for the people; it makes the nation prosperous, suppresses traitors, and promotes talented men. It sympathizes with the direction in which the people are progressing. Abroad it maintains trust with foreign nations, and at home it saves the people from natural disasters. Look at the example of George Washington, the founder of the American nation. He deserves our respect and admiration because, after having given meritorious service to the nation, he did not keep his office as a private possession; moreover, he was able to bequeath peace and stability to the new nation. The reason the shogunate lacks authority is because of its own selfish ambitions. The reason the shogunate cannot suppress evil men is because of its failure to adhere to just principles. Shogunal authority does not simply depend on the army's size or the treasury's wealth. That is why I maintain that supreme authority in the nation must, in the end, return to just principles.

Wicked men now fill the streets of Edo, men who adhere to evil customs, selfish men, robbers and thieves, angry grudge-ridden men. Everywhere there is confusion; there is no telling what will happen next. Whether these men, whose emergence appears unstoppable, may be the foundation of the future and from whom heroes may be born, I do not know. I have my opinion, but I will not divulge it. Intelligent men will understand me. The samurai in Edo hate the fact that the western daimyo [Satsuma and Chōshū] do not adhere to their views; they are afraid of anyone who opposes them. They do not understand the general situation of the nation. Although the [southwestern] daimyo may rebel and plot treasonous acts, success will not be theirs. Moreover, there are no great men among them at this time; they all hold narrow, selfish views and have forgotten about public, enlightened, and just principles. If they should launch a violent rebellion, those under them will rise up against their masters. It is clear to me that these powerful daimyo do not merit fear. Nonetheless, the shogunate is gathering the daimyo of small domains like a flock of sheep and urging them to attack the [southwestern] daimyo. This is something that will only invite national collapse. Such narrow-mindedness! The more one gathers, the more its value decreases. Will this not cause fellow countrymen to fight among themselves?

Moreover, the people will become alienated from their rulers. If, in the future, there are those who divest the daimyo of their rank, they will appear from the poor and propertyless class of the common people, if not the stable master at a way station, a sandal bearer. The daimyo and nobles of today do not do their own work, but rather sit and receive benefits from the work of others. From the time of their birth they need do nothing for themselves. A servant tucks them into bed; they neither grow nor weave; all their life's needs are taken care of by members of the lower classes. This not being enough, they levy heavy taxes on the lower classes and suck their sweat and blood. Is this the proper way for leaders to behave? It is easy to see that the alienation of people's minds will increase day by day. Although status morality has not yet collapsed, it is only a matter of time. This is something that deserves deep consideration.

About ten years ago Tokugawa Nariaki, a man of extraordinary disposition, promoted a movement to "revere the emperor and expel the barbarians" as a means to awaken the daimyo from their deep sleep. At that time, the shogunate thought such a policy to be wise, but not realistic; it was feared that war would result and so it was not carried out. Thereafter the nation has been in chaos and voices of condemnation have arisen incessantly. This is because of the government's narrow-mindedness and its inability to understand the true nature of the "revere the emperor, expel the barbarians" movement. A great deal of harm resulted when that policy was not fully implemented. The harm, however, was not the fault of Nariaki's ideas; rather it was due to reluctance and indecisiveness. Therefore, who are we to blame?

Since then there have been no great, wise, and discerning men in the nation; all are indecisive and drunk on the notion of revering the emperor and expelling the barbarians. No one is sober. Those who argued over the differences between "closed country" and "open country" were narrow-minded, as are those who today argue over the pros and cons of government by assembly. Upon reflection it is clear that the knowledge and awareness of the Japanese people have increased. We can forecast the future while sitting in our seats: From this point on, if the knowledge and awareness of the people continually progresses, righteousness and justice will suffice to govern them. Casting aside all political stratagems, we can sit back with our arms folded and with sincerity, enlightenment, and justice carry out a national renovation. The way a retainer establishes himself in the world is through his duty to assist his lord in his heavenly office of nurturing the people and keeping law and order in the nation. All battles fought without such a perception will necessarily fail. The present age is one in which the retainers are not content to live peacefully on their stipend. They enact heavy taxes, cause suffering to the people and beg the townsmen for assistance. Those who have office promote only those who flatter them and shun all who would oppose them. Now, our lord Yoshinobu, with an unparalleled attitude of great farsightedness, is attempting to rectify the nation. However, not realizing this, there are those who obstruct our lord's great plan with their own petty selfish desires. Truthfully, the resentment and grief are more than I can bear. All I ask is that these selfish desires be discarded and that justice be given due consideration.

[Signed] Kaishū the madman

30

Satirical Poem at the Time of the Surrender of Edo Castle

May 3, 1868

Once the former shogun Tokugawa Yoshinobu had been declared an "enemy of the court," his capital of Edo became the target of forces fighting under the imperial banner. Hampered by the need to wait for reinforcements and a lack of funds, these armies moved so slowly that Tokugawa sympathizers had time to petition the court for leniency. Tenshō-in, the widow of the thirteenth shogun, and originally from Satsuma, announced that she would never leave the castle. The widow of the fourteenth, the new emperor's aunt Kazunomiya, sent her chief female attendant to her kinsmen with pleas for mercy. Finally, in a famous series of meetings on the outskirts of Edo on April 5 and 6, 1868, Saigō Takamori, the commander of the imperial forces, and Katsu Kaishū, in overall

M. William Steele, *Alternative Narratives in Modern Japanese History* (London: RoutledgeCurzon, 2003), 76.

command of Edo, saved the city from the fires of war by negotiating the castle's surrender.

Commoners' disenchantment with Tokugawa rule was palpable. Already they had jeered at what they perceived as Yoshinobu's ineptitude and cowardice in satirical prints and songs. At the same time, they hardly welcomed their new rulers. A satirical compendium current at the time suggests that neither side found favor with them.

Are we afraid of being called an enemy of the court? NO!
Is there a way to escape humble submission? NO!
Does the emperor know anything? NO!
Is honor due to the pseudo-princes? NO!
Is respect due to wearers of imperial headbands? NO!
Does the wicked army have any money? NO!
Does wisdom exist among our leaders? NO!
Does righteousness exist between high and low? NO!
Is there a path leading to loyalty and fealty, benevolence and
    virtue? NO!

31

SHINAGAWA YAJIRŌ

"Miya-san, Miya-san": A Popular Marching Song
1868

After the defeat of Tokugawa forces at Toba Fushimi, which marked the beginning of the Boshin Civil War, a court order issued on February 3 charged Yoshinobu with treason, labeled him an "enemy of the court," and urged an attack on his domains. An imperial army, organized in three divisions and numbering some fifty thousand men, began the march on Edo on March 2. Appointed the supreme commander of the eastern campaign, imperial prince Arisugawa Taruhito carried the imperial sword and the

---

Inoue Takeshi, ed., *Nihon shōka zenshū* (Tokyo: Ongaku no Tomo-sha, 1993), 15; "Boshin kangun shingun uta utsushi," manuscript in Akita Kenritsu Kōmonjokan: Ono 7369, translated by M. William Steele and Anne Walthall.

imperial banner, both of which the emperor had personally handed to him. The army marched to the beat of a military song attributed to Shinagawa Yajirō (1843–1900), a disciple of Yoshida Shōin (Document 10) with a long history of pro-imperial activism. In 1862 he led an attack on the British legation in Edo; in 1864 he joined Maki Izumi and other loyalists in Chōshū's ill-fated attack on Kyoto (Document 19). The imperial sword, the imperial banner, and the "Miya-san, Miya-san" marching song urged the imperial troops on to victory and served as powerful symbols lending legitimacy in the eyes of common people to the use of military force to destroy the old regime and set up a new imperial government.

In addition to a translation of the standard version of the song, we include a sexually suggestive version from Akita, in northeastern Japan. The original continued well into the twentieth century as the first in a long tradition of patriotic war songs. It was also incorporated into Gilbert and Sullivan's 1885 operetta, The Mikado, *and the "Miya-san" melody can be heard in Puccini's* Madame Butterfly.

Standard Version

Lord Above, Lord Above
What's that fluttering in front of your noble horse?
Tokotonyare tonyare-na

Know you not?
It's the imperial brocade banner
Urging us to punish enemies of the court.
Tokotonyare tonyare-na

Make war upon those who oppose
Our emperor who rules over all under heaven.
Tokotonyare tonyare-na

Do not miss your mark! Keep firing!
O men from Satsuma, Chōshū, and Tosa.
Tokotonyare tonyare-na

On the battlefields
Fushimi, Toba, Hashimoto, and Kuzuha.
Tokotonyare tonyare-na

No one can equal
We men from Satsuma, Chōshū, Tosa, and Hizen.
Tokotonyare tonyare-na

You famous warriors of the Kanto!
Where oh where have you fled?
Tokotonyare tonyare-na

Giving up your castle and afraid to fight
Have you fled farther to the east?
Tokotonyare tonyare-na

To invade other lands and kill their people
Is no man's desire.
Tokotonyare tonyare-na

But attack them we will if they resist
We men from Satsuma, Chōshū and Tosa.
Tokotonyare tonyare-na

Just like falling rain, bullets come pelting at us
With no thought for our lives.
Tokotonyare tonyare-na

We vie for the lead, everyone
For the sake of our lord.
Tokotonyare tonyare-na

Akita Version

Lord Above, Lord Above
What's that fluttering in front of your noble horse?
Tokotonyare tonyare-na

Know you not?
It's the imperial brocade banner
Urging us to punish enemies of the court.
Tokotonyare tonyare-na

On each side wave banners of the gods and Buddhas.
Tokotonyare tonyare-na

Just like falling rain, bullets come pelting at us.
Tokotonyare tonyare-na

With no thought for our lives
We vie for the lead, everyone
For the sake of our lord.
Tokotonyare tonyare-na

Young girl, Oh young girl
What's that fluttering in front of you?
Tokotonyare tonyare-na

Know you not?
It's a tie-dyed yukata [light summer robe]
Tempting the desires of our customers.
Tokotonyare tonyare-na

32

Women of Aizu

October 1868

From the beginning of the Boshin Civil War, the Aizu domain was a major target of imperial forces. Matsudaira Katamori, the Aizu daimyo, had taken charge of suppressing rabble-rousers in Kyoto on behalf of the shogun, earning him the animosity of the men from Satsuma and Chōshū and other pro-imperial groups. After the surrender of Edo Castle in May 1868, Aizu joined Sendai, Yonezawa, and others in a league of northeastern domains to continue the resistance against the new government. During the summer and early autumn, most members of the league were either defeated militarily or forced to surrender.

The battle against Aizu that began in early October was especially fierce. Katamori urged his samurai to "fight to the death to wipe out the stain on the domain's honor."[1] By the time Aizu-Wakamatsu Castle fell on November 6, some 2,557 of the domain's defenders had died, many by suicide. That number includes the 197 women who died fighting, but it does not include the 230 noncombatants—women, children, and elderly men—who took their own lives.

Published in women's journals at the end of the nineteenth century, these reminiscences are from women who were in their teens or twenties in 1868. In addition, Saigō Tanomo, a senior adviser to Katamori,

---

[1]Ishimitsu Mahito, ed., *Remembering Aizu: The Testament of Shiba Gorō,* trans. Teruko Craig (Honolulu: University of Hawai'i Press, 1999), 15.

Miyazaki Tomihachi, ed., *Aizu Boshin sensō shiryōshū* (Tokyo: Shinjinbutsu Ōraisha, 1991), 165–69, 177–78, 185–87, 296–97. Translated by Anne Walthall.

*recalls what his womenfolk did. The Aizu women's commitment to the
code of the warrior reveals much about Japanese thought and behavior
at the time of the Meiji Restoration.*

Yamakawa Misako, age seventeen: While shut up inside the castle,
we women made cartridges and prepared rice balls as rations for the soldiers. To make the cartridges, we took a small piece of paper and wrapped
it around a narrow bamboo tube. We then twisted a bit of the paper to
make the bottom and pulled out the bamboo. We placed the bullet inside,
poured gunpowder over the top, and then twisted the top tightly. Once a
number of cartridges had been laid out, ten- to twelve-year-old children
picked them up and carried them to the soldiers who were fighting with
all their might.

We were really short of food. Since white rice doesn't store well, there
was nothing inside the castle aside from brown. We had no time to thresh
or simmer it; we simply boiled water in a big pot, poured in the rice, and
stirred it around a bit. We then took the hot rice and made rice balls. The
rice was so hot that it peeled the skin off our hands. At first we too ate the
brown rice, but when it started to run out, women and children were no
longer allowed to eat it in order to leave enough for the soldiers. Instead
we were fed with rice flour that had been stored for a very long time.
This too was cooked by boiling water, then pouring in the flour and stir-
ring. Once it became the consistency of glue, we ate it. Under ordinary
circumstances, it wasn't so bad, but because it was so old that no one
knew how long it had been stored, bugs had eaten it and left their husks.
When we poured it in the hot water, we found lots of bug shells and other
things that looked like naked bugs. These we pulled out one by one while
we ate. We had no time to think about how dirty or disgusting it was. You
have no idea how much we appreciated the brown rice with all its husks
or the old rice flour mixed with bugs.

In addition to making bullets and fixing rice balls, we women had the
great responsibility of caring for the wounded. Thinking that the castle
might collapse under the reverberation of the cannon, we brought them
all covered with blood into the women's quarters. Every time we saw
one, we choked back tears, thinking, alas, another man on our side has
fallen. Although there were several doctors, we had little by way of medi-
cine and other supplies so that all we could do for the wounded was offer
consolation.

One bullet pierced my sister-in-law from shin to thigh, another hit her
side, another her shoulder, and another her cheek. . . . Because there

was no time to bury the dead, in most cases they were tearfully placed in a dry well. For my sister-in-law, however, because my elder brother had lots of troops under his command, her corpse was placed in a casket and respectfully buried.

The cannonballs were round, about the size of a child's head. If they fell without bursting on the roof, they made a sputtering sound and caught fire. Because it would have been a catastrophe for fire to erupt inside the castle, the women would soak bedding and clothing in water, climb barefoot up to the roof, and put out the fire. When the children saw this, they ran up and down shouting in excitement.

Because we were resolved to die, we took no money into the castle. Instead we carried sharp implements and good swords. I did not have a dagger. Instead I had a long sword suitable for killing people. If I was going to die, I thought it would be a bore to die by my own hand. I wanted to be killed honorably while striking the enemy. However I was never allowed to do that because to put women into battle would have reflected badly on our lord's name.

Niijima Yaeko, age twenty-four: Since the men in my natal house served as gunnery instructors for the Aizu lord, everyone went into the castle. I put on male clothing with *hakama* over my kimono, and I went along too, wearing straw sandals, with two swords at my hip, and carrying a seven-shot repeating American-made Spencer carbine. Other women carried halberds. That spring my younger brother Saburō had died in the Toba battle in Yamashiro. I wore his clothing in remembrance of him, with the feeling that I had become Saburō and I must kill his enemies. Resolved to fight so long as I had life for the sake of my lord and for the sake of my younger brother, I entered the castle.

As Yamakawa Misako said [in the previous selection], the duties for women who entered the castle were to cook rations, make bullets, and tend the wounded. While we were working in this fashion, what worried us most—well this is a little indelicate—was about going to the toilet. As women of warrior families, for us to die like dogs without getting back at the enemy would have been shameful for our lord and for our family's honor. For that reason, we were resolved to meet a splendid end and to fight as hard as we could. On the other hand, should we be in the toilet when it was destroyed by a cannonball and we meet our end in such a fashion, for a woman this would have been the most shameful disgrace.

Mizushima Kikuko, age twenty: At the beginning of October, the defenses at Takizawa Hill [outside the city] collapsed, cannonballs came boom, boom, and fires started. On the eighth, our house, which was on the edge of the castle town, burned. We dressed ourselves, and carrying our halberds and our swords, with extra weapons stuffed into our belts, we retreated. My sister and I planned to enter the castle, but the gate was already shut. We could do nothing but retreat again when we ran into Nakano Takeko with her mother and sisters. Okamura Sumako too came along, and that is how we formed the woman's brigade. . . .

Late the next night, I heard whispering. When I listened closely, I learned that Nakano Takeko and her mother were planning to kill Yūko. The three Nakano women were beautiful beyond compare, and the sixteen-year-old Yūko was not only the youngest but also a rare and wonderful beauty. Should she fall into enemy hands and be treated as their plaything, it would be a disgrace. The discussion was about how it would be better to kill her that night. My sister and I jumped up and tried to stop them. Finally they gave up the idea.

The next morning, the tenth, all of us in the woman's brigade cut our hair so short that we looked like men. At dusk we arrived at the Bridge of Tears [near the execution ground] where fighting had already broken out. From the beginning men had opposed sending our women's brigade to the front because it would be shameful for it to appear that Aizu was in such trouble that it had to rely on women. Even though the fighting had commenced, the men tried to stop us by saying "Don't go, don't go," and that meant that we were not able to fight as much as we would have liked. Nonetheless, we managed to thrust [at the enemy] with our halberds. At that time Nakano Takeko, her mother Kōko, and especially the young Yūko who had caused us so much worry did really splendid deeds. Alas, Takeko died, having been struck in the forehead by a bullet that came directly at her.

Her sister Yūko told her mother, "To make sure my sister's head does not fall into enemy hands, I'm going to cut it off." While staving off the enemy, she got to where her sister had fallen, cut off her head, and wrapped it in her white silk headband. The head was later buried at Hōkai temple in Bange, and a man from Kaga erected a stone monument for it.

Saigō Tanomo, former house elder: For my mother and the rest of my family to have killed themselves while I was on duty on October 8 stays in my gut to this day. . . . I remember that my mother's death poem consisted of a reworking of one that my father had written on the occasion of a party at our house when each guest had contributed a couplet in Chinese. "The autumn frost flies away, and the autumn wind blows cold. / Once the white clouds leave, the moon rises high." It was typical of an old person but it did not sound like one written by a woman. [It was written in Chinese.] . . . She was fifty-eight at the time. My wife Chieko was thirty-four. For her death poem she wrote: "Even with a body / entrusted to the wind / like slender bamboo / there have to be / joints that do not bend." As might be expected, it was finely crafted. My younger sister Mijuko had always had a brave heart. "Each time / that I return from the dead / and I am born in this world / I will become a brave warrior." She was twenty-six. . . . My thirteen-year-old daughter Hōfuko wrote, "If you take my hand / and we go together, / I won't get lost," and her sixteen-year-old sister Saifuko finished it for her: "When the time comes, I will take it / as we depart for death on the mountain road," a charmingly unaffected verse. [Of my younger daughters,] Tazuruko was nine, Tokiwako was four, Sueko was two. [The others who died:] In addition to the couple from a branch of the Saigō family, there was also the Komori family, who had left the Edo mansion that spring to live with us. There were five of them, including the maternal grandmother. There were three in Machita Denpachi's family. . . . When I think of what happened to the young children, I feel such pity.

6

Toward a New Japan

33

The Charter Oath and Injunctions to Commoners
April 6, 1868

*Proclaimed in a solemn ceremony within the Kyoto Imperial Palace on
April 6, 1868, the Charter Oath was an important foundational document for the new imperial government. It promised democratic and social
reforms and the need to open the country to the outside world. But it
represented more than a set of guiding principles. It may have convinced
some daimyo, skeptical of the "revere the emperor, expel the barbarians"
roots of the imperial restoration, that the new regime would be a progressive one. Others envisioned a return to ancient times and a closed-country
policy or remained sympathetic to the Tokugawa family. The men who
represented the various factions around the emperor—Kido Takayoshi
(Chōshū), Ōkubo Toshimichi (Satsuma), and the court noble Iwakura
Tomomi—feared internal squabbling as much as they did resistance by
pro-Tokugawa troops. Having the emperor proclaim the oath to the gods
of heaven and earth in front of the assembled leaders in the new regime
and then commanding them, one by one, to affix their names to the pledge
clarified goals and ensured their commitment to the new imperial order.*

*The next day, the new government issued injunctions for commoners
designed to replace those of the discredited Tokugawa shogunate. They
gave no hint of the progressive goals outlined in the oath. While acknowl-
edging that the imperial government would recognize foreign treaties,
they restated Tokugawa prescriptions encouraging ethical conduct and*

John Breen, "The Imperial Oath of April 1868: Ritual, Politics, and Power in the Restoration," *Monumenta Nipponica* 51, no. 4 (Winter 1996): 410, 412; *Meiji Japan through
Contemporary Sources*, vol. 2, *1844–1882* (Tokyo: Centre for East Asian Cultural Studies,
1970), 74–76.

the strict observance of the law. Christianity, for example, would continue to be outlawed until 1873.

The Charter Oath in Five Articles

Item. We shall determine all matters of state by public discussion, after assemblies have been convoked far and wide.

Item. We shall unite the hearts and minds of people high and low, the better to pursue with vigor the rule of the realm.

Item. We are duty bound to ensure that all people, nobility, military, and commoners too, may fulfill their aspirations and not yield to despair.

Item. We shall break through the shackles of former evil practice and base our actions on the principles of international law.

Item. We shall see knowledge throughout the world and thus invigorate the foundations of this imperial nation.

My [Emperor Meiji] intention is to implement reform the likes of which have never before been seen. I have, therefore, seized the initiative; I have sworn an oath before the gods of heaven and earth; I have set forth our national goals, and I hope thus, to establish a path of safety for all my subjects. May you be inspired by this initiative. Unite your hearts and be unsparing in your efforts. . . .

Notification of the Five Injunctions, April 7, 1868

FIRST INJUNCTION

People are duly to follow the five ethical pathways of man.

People are to be kind to those who are solitary and helpless, or seriously suffering from illness.

People are not to commit crimes such as murder, arson, or theft of another's property.

SECOND INJUNCTION

Those who gather for the purpose of evil are, without excuse, regarded as "conspirators"; planning to appeal forcibly to the officers along with conspirators is to be called a "petition by force"; [illegally] leaving the town or village of domicile by mutual agreement among only themselves is to be termed "flight"; the above activities are all prohibited. If any such actions take place, people should report it immediately to the office concerned. The reporter will be duly rewarded.

THIRD INJUNCTION

The Christian creed is strictly prohibited. If one finds anybody suspected of the above, he is to report to the office concerned, and will be duly rewarded.

FOURTH INJUNCTION

Now that changes have taken place in our imperial rule, the government has, in accord with venerable principles, proposed to start communications with foreign countries, and various affairs are to be dealt with immediately by the Imperial Court. While the government is to observe the treaties in accordance with international law, people throughout the country are here reminded duly to follow the imperial orders and never to commit offenses [in violation of the above matters]. They are reminded that from now on those who arbitrarily kill foreigners or commit any crimes of the sort are not only violating the imperial order and putting the country in trouble, but also causing the venerable honor of our imperial country seriously to lose face in the eyes of every foreign country which has proposed to have official relations with us. Since the above betrayal cannot be excused, even those who are of samurai rank are to be deprived of their rank and duly punished according to the relative gravity of the crime. Every person is thus reminded to observe the above imperial order firmly, and not to commit unreasonable violence of any sort.

FIFTH INJUNCTION

Since changes have taken place in our imperial rule, venerable measures are now being taken to let the land enjoy peace as soon as possible, and to enable the people to feel tranquil and to occupy their proper places. In such a situation absolutely no one wandering around the country is to be excused. It is only natural that any "flight" from one's part of the country without proper reasons, whether by samurai or not, is in view of current developments strictly prohibited. If a person runs away from his part of the country and commits criminal deeds, the fault will be his master's. However, since times have changed now, if a person, regardless of his rank, wishes to make a representation for the sake of the imperial country or his master, the government would provide him the means to do so, and let him fully discuss the problem with an easy mind. Such a person, therefore, is reminded to make application to the Council of Ministers.

Consequently, from now on, all those who employ workers, whether they be samurai, farmers or merchants, are to make thorough investigation into the worker's previous status. In case one employs a person who is guilty of a "flight," or has caused a disturbance, the fault will naturally lie with the master.

34

KIDO TAKAYOSHI

Abolition of Domains and Creation of Prefectures

1871

Following victory in the Boshin Civil War, the Meiji emperor moved to Edo, renamed Tokyo on September 3, to inaugurate his reign. Nonetheless, Japan remained fragmented into nearly three hundred principalities. The daimyo's symbolic return of their land and population registers to the emperor in March 1869 marked the first step in a delicate process that led to the centralization of political, economic, and military authority, but a new system of domain governors (former daimyo) only caused confusion. Many governors and their retainers continued to place local interests over those of the center. Early in 1870, the small group of self-selected men from Satsuma, Chōshū, Tosa, and Hizen who ruled in the emperor's name sought to prohibit the domains from borrowing money from overseas in an effort to make foreign affairs the monopoly of the central government. Not all obeyed.

The final push against fragmentation came in the summer of 1871. Fully aware of the difficulty of corralling the domains, Chōshū's Kido Takayoshi composed an imperial edict that abolished the domains and replaced them with prefectures, redrawing Japan's political map in the name of bureaucratic efficiency and national unity. The new system consisted of seventy-two prefectures, three municipal districts, and one special government for Hokkaido. Replaced by men appointed by the center, the former hereditary governors were obliged to reside in Tokyo. All domain military forces were disbanded. In contrast to the Meiji Restoration, this

---

Sidney Devere Brown and Akiko Hirota, trans., *The Diary of Kido Takayoshi*, vol. 2, *1871–1874* (Tokyo: University of Tokyo Press, 1985), 48, 55–56, 57, 60, 63, 64–65, 68–69; W. W. McLaren, "Japanese Government Documents," *Transactions of the Asiatic Society of Japan* 42, no. 1 (1914): 32–33.

event may be termed the Meiji Revolution. The old military regime was dead, replaced by a government centered in a single authority, the emperor.

Excerpts from Kido Takayoshi's Diary

28 July 1871. . . . Nearly 10,000 soldiers have been summoned recently from Satsuma, Chōshū, and Tosa as an Imperial Guard to protect the Imperial Government and to assist in establishing a foundation for it; therefore, I hope that the three domains will abide by the Imperial wishes without fail, exert themselves to bring the nation under a single authority, and fix the course of all the domains along a common path. That is to say: the Return of the Registers to the Throne was the first step; and we must now strive toward the second step, giving reality to the Return of the Registers, and unifying the nation. . . . Although the new system has been decided on, the general run of people in the land do not obey central government orders.

13 August 1871. . . . Since last night I have been thinking over the way the present reform program is developing; and everything about it is at odds with what I proposed repeatedly when I accepted this office. . . . If a foundation for the government is not firmly agreed to, and the jurisdictions and regulations of the several ministries not decided, how can we rule the country? When I think about it, I believe that we were on the brink of disaster today.

15 August 1871. . . . As I have become worried about any delay in the matter which we have had under consideration these past several days, I had a heated argument with Lord Iwakura, reproached Prince Sanjō for being about to lose the opportunity, and explained to Saigō [Takamori] again the main purpose of the new system. Finally at 2 today we reached a decision to implement it.

22 August 1871. . . . Three years ago, as I observed the general trend of the times, I hoped to demolish the seven-hundred-year-old feudal structure completely, give the names of counties and prefectures to the local units of government, gradually unite the strength of the nation, and nurture men of talent. I made a great effort on behalf of this plan; and I talked with several of my colleagues about it. But no more than one of them gave ready assent to it. Inevitably I had to resort to a stratagem to persuade them by arguing that we should abolish the ranks established by the vermilion seal orders of the old shogunate, and to return the fiefs granted by it to the Imperial Government. Permission to retain them or not would derive from Imperial orders; and thereby the correct relationship between sovereign and subject would be forthcoming. Finally Ōkubo [Toshimichi] of Satsuma and others agreed to this; and the Return of the Registers to the Emperor was carried out. This stirred up great controversy; and some of those who perceived that the plan was mainly mine were of a mind to assassinate me. People in my own domain reviled me for the most part, and even a good many of those who worked for the Restoration cause argued against my plan.

27 August 1871. . . . I went to the Palace at 8; Saigō, Ōkubo, and I held a secret conference for starting to implement our plan. Each of us had objections to certain parts of it. Carrying out such a major undertaking, leaving everybody satisfied, is extremely difficult; so we decided on the vital points first, leaving the details for discussion at some later date. Thereupon Saigō and I reported our plan to Prince Sanjō, asking him to report it to the Throne and obtain permission for it promptly.

29 August 1871. . . . At 2 the Emperor appeared in the Grand Hall, and the governors of fifty-six domains were summoned before him. There the Imperial edict on the abolition of the domains was read to them, and the governors were all dismissed from their offices. With this, the seven-hundred-year-old political structure, with all of its undesirable features, has been reformed; and we may say that the foundation for a structure which will enable us to face the nations of the world on a basis of equality for the first time has been established. At the time of the Restoration the several domains moved from the battles around Kyoto to continue fighting in the northeast; and after a year had passed, the whole country was pacified. But then the domains began to compete with each other. Satsuma watched Chōshū, and Tosa eyed Hizen, and all focused their attention exclusively on affairs within Japan; but failed to notice trends in the world at some distance from us, or to prepare countermeasures to deal with the powers of the world. The Imperial Government had little strength while each domain had its own feelings about the matter. Some advocated excluding the foreigners; others wanted to close the country; and still others favored fully opening the country. If we were not farsighted enough to bring unity out of this confusion, the collapse of the nation would have come without waiting many more days.

3 September 1871. . . . The plan for the new central government structure was finally approved today; and this will take care of the matter of regulations for the ministries. In the past, regrettably, government officials were apt to make decisions, not on the basis of whether they were right or wrong, but in accordance with how the voices of the majority were, as they sought to gain public favor. A great many plans were made in that way. I have worried about this situation for many years; but things were not done as I wished.

Imperial Edict on the Abolition of the Domains and the Creation of Prefectures

We are of the opinion that in a time of radical reform like the present, if We desire by its means to give protection and tranquility to the people at home, and abroad to maintain equality with foreign nations, words must be made to mean in reality what they claim to signify, and the government of the country must center in a single authority.

Some time ago We gave Our sanction to the scheme by which all the clans [daimyo] restored to Us their registers. We appointed governors for the first time, each to perform the duties of his office.

But owing to the lengthened endurance of the old system during several hundred years, there have been cases where the word only was pronounced and the reality not performed. How is it possible for Us, under such circumstances, to give protection and tranquility to the people, and to maintain equality with foreign nations?

Profoundly regretting this condition of affairs, We now completely abolish the domains and convert them into prefectures, with the object of diligently retrenching expenditure and of arriving at convenience of working, of getting rid of the unreality of names and of abolishing the disease of government proceeding from multiform centers.

Do ye, Our assembled servants, take well to heart this Our will.

August 29, 1871

35

ITŌ HIROBUMI

Speech on Japan's Future
January 18, 1872

Soon after the establishment of prefectures, Japan's leaders left routine affairs in the hands of a caretaker government while they went on a lengthy study tour, called the Iwakura mission, to examine modern institutions in Europe and the United States. The plan was to grasp firsthand the realities of the world and formulate a program for the radical reform of Japanese political and economic life. In San Francisco, the first stop, vice envoy Itō Hirobumi (1841–1909) gave a speech in which he declared that Japan's future depended on learning from the West but at the same time hinted that Japan would not be content to be forever the West's inferior. The Iwakura mission was but the starting point for Japan's Rising Sun flag, the Hinomaru, to rise forever "onward and upward among the enlightened nations of the world."

A Meiji period oligarch and drafter of the 1889 Meiji Constitution, Itō was one of the first Japanese to study overseas. Born in Chōshū to a family that was barely of samurai status, he studied under Yoshida Shōin (Document 10). In 1863, realizing the dream of his teacher, he entered University College London intent on discovering the roots of Western wealth and power. He returned to Japan committed to both the imperial cause and a determined program of westernization. After the Meiji Restoration, his firsthand knowledge of the West allowed him to advance quickly up the ranks of the new imperial government.

Gentlemen: Being honored by your kind generosity, I gladly express to you, and through you to the citizens of San Francisco, our heartfelt gratitude for the friendly reception, which has everywhere greeted the Embassy since its arrival in your State, and especially for the marked compliment paid this evening to our nation.

Charles Lanman, *The Japanese in America* (New York: University Publishing Company, 1872), 13–16.

This is perhaps a fitting opportunity to give a brief and reliable outline of many improvements being introduced into Japan. Few but native Japanese have any correct knowledge of our country's internal condition.

Friendly intercourse with the Treaty powers has been maintained (first among which was the United States), and a good understanding on the part of our people has increased commercial relations. Our mission, under special instruction from His Majesty, the Emperor, while seeking to protect the rights and interests of our respective nations, will seek to unite them more closely in the future, convinced that we shall appreciate each other more when we know each other better.

By reading, hearing, and by observation in foreign lands, our people have acquired a general knowledge of constitutions, habits, and manners, as they exist in most foreign countries. Foreign customs are now generally understood throughout Japan.

Today it is the earnest wish of both our Government and people to strive for the highest points of civilization enjoyed by more enlightened countries. Looking to this end we have adopted their military, naval, scientific, and educational institutions, and knowledge has flowed to us freely in the wake of foreign commerce. Although our improvement has been rapid in material civilization, the mental improvement of our people has been far greater. Our wisest men, after careful observation, agree in this opinion.

While held in absolute obedience by despotic sovereigns through many thousand years, our people knew no freedom or liberty of thought. With our material improvement, they learned to understand their rightful privileges, which, for ages, have been denied them. Civil war was but a temporary result.

Our Daimyos magnanimously surrendered their principalities, and their voluntary action was accepted by the general Government. Within a year a feudal system, firmly established many centuries ago, has been completely abolished, without firing a gun or shedding a drop of blood. These wonderful results have been accomplished by the united action of a Government and people, now pressing jointly forward in the peaceful paths of progress. What country in the middle ages broke down its feudal system without war?

These facts assure us that mental changes in Japan exceed even the material improvements. By educating our women, we hope to insure greater intelligence in future generations. With this end in view, our maidens have already commenced to come to you for their education.

Japan cannot claim originality as yet, but it will aim to exercise practical wisdom by adopting the advantages, and avoiding the errors taught her by the history of those enlightened nations whose experience is her teacher. Scarcely a year ago, I examined minutely the financial system of the United States, and, while in Washington, received most valuable assistance from distinguished officers of your Treasury Department. Every detail learned was faithfully reported to my Government, and suggestions then made have been adopted, and some of them are now already in practical operation.

In the Department of Public Works, now under my administration, the progress has been satisfactory. Railroads are being built, both in the eastern and western portions of the Empire. Telegraph wires are stretching over many hundred miles of our territory, and nearly one thousand miles will be completed within a few months. Lighthouses now line our coasts, and our shipyards are active. All these assist our civilization, and we fully acknowledge our indebtedness to you and other foreign nations.

As Ambassadors and as men, our greatest hope is to return from this mission laden with results—valuable to our beloved country and calculated to advance permanently her material and intellectual condition. While in duty bound to protect the rights and privileges of our people, we shall aim to increase our commerce, and, by a corresponding increase of our productions, hope to create a healthy basis for this greater activity.

As distinguished citizens of a great commercial nation, preparing for business, desirous of participating in the new commercial era now dawning auspiciously upon the Pacific, Japan offers you her hearty cooperation.

Your modern inventions and results of accumulated knowledge, enable you to do more in days than our fathers accomplished in years. Time, so condensed with precious opportunities, we can ill afford to waste. Japan is anxious to press forward.

The red disc in the center of our national flag shall no longer appear like a wafer over a sealed empire, but henceforth be in fact what it is designed to be, the noble emblem of the rising sun, moving onward and upward amid the enlightened nations of the world.

A Chronology of Events Leading
to the Meiji Restoration
(1792–1871)

1792   *October 18*   Russian envoy Adam Laxman arrives in Hokkaido with requests for trade.

1808   *October 4*   British frigate *Phaeton* arrives in Nagasaki in search of Dutch ships; lands troops and demands supplies, and then sails off.

1823–
1824   British sailors land in Japan in search of food.

1825   *April 6*   Shogunate issues order to drive off foreigners using force.

1833–
1837   Famine throughout Japan.

1837   *March 25*   Former police inspector Ōshio Heihachirō launches rebellion to save poor in Osaka.

1841–
1842   Economic and social reforms announced by shogunate.

1853   *July 8*   U.S. commodore Matthew Perry arrives at outer entrance to Edo Bay to establish relations with Japan.

1854   *March 31*   Treaty of Kanagawa between Japan and United States.

1858   *July 29*   Treaty of Amity and Commerce, first commercial treaty between Japan and United States.

1859   Purge of shogunate's critics; Yoshida Shōin and others executed on November 21.

1860   *March 24*   Assassination of shogun's chief councilor, Ii Naosuke.

1861   *December 16*   Emperor's half-sister, Princess Kazunomiya, arrives in Edo to marry Shogun Iemochi in an attempt to bring together court and military.

1862   *June–October*   Reform of relations between shogun and daimyo.

September 14   Shanghai-based merchant Charles Richardson killed by Satsuma samurai.

1863   *April 9*   Wooden statues of Ashikaga shoguns beheaded as warning to contemporary traitors.

April 21   Shogun Iemochi arrives in Kyoto.

June 25   Date set for shogunate's expulsion of the barbarians.

1864   *Summer*   Civil war erupts in Mito.

August 20   Chōshū troops attack Kyoto.

August 25   Shogunate orders first punitive expedition against Chōshū domain.

December 9   Chōshū surrenders to shogunate.

1865   *May 6*   Shogunate orders second punitive expedition against Chōshū.

1866   *July 10*   Commoners riot in Edo.

July 18   Outbreak of hostilities between shogunate and Chōshū.

July 24–31   Major outburst of violence in hinterlands north of Edo.

1867   *February 13*   Prince Mutsuhito becomes Emperor Meiji.

March–April   Shogun Yoshinobu meets with French ambassador Léon Roches in Osaka to initiate plans for strengthening shogunate.

July 23   Tosa and Satsuma men agree to act jointly in forcing shogun to return governing authority to imperial court.

August   *Ee ja nai ka* craze begins in central Japan and spreads up and down eastern seaboard.

October 15   Satsuma and Chōshū conclude agreement to work together to overthrow Tokugawa regime — by force if necessary.

October 29   Former Tosa daimyo Yamauchi Toyoshige submits memorial to shogun requesting that governing authority be returned to imperial court.

November 8   Secret imperial decrees request Chōshū and Satsuma domains to overthrow Tokugawa shogunate.

November 9   Yoshinobu offers to return governing authority to imperial court; court accepts offer next day.

December 10   Activist and visionary Sakamoto Ryōma killed by Tokugawa agents in Kyoto.

1868   *January 3*   Troops from Satsuma, Echizen, Tosa, and Hizen domains seize imperial palace and declare restoration of direct imperial rule.

January 19 Troops from former shogunate attack and burn down residence of Satsuma daimyo in Edo.

January 27 Chōshū and Satsuma forces engage troops loyal to Tokugawa family at Toba-Fushimi, on outskirts of Kyoto. Beginning of Boshin Civil War.

February 3 Yoshinobu termed "enemy of the court" and stripped of court rank; lands confiscated and placed under direct control of imperial court.

February 8 New minister of foreign affairs meets with foreign representatives in Hyōgo to announce inauguration of new imperial regime.

March 2 Imperial army departs Kyoto to subdue Yoshinobu.

April 5–6 Katsu Kaishū (Tokugawa forces) and Saigō Takamori (imperial army) negotiate surrender of Edo.

April 6 Charter Oath issued.

May 3 Edo Castle surrendered to imperial army; Yoshinobu departs Edo for Mito, where he enters confinement.

July 4 Battle of Ueno Hill; imperial army gains control of Edo.

September 3 Name of Edo changed to Tokyo (Eastern Capital)

October 4 Former commander of Tokugawa navy Enomoto Takeaki escapes Tokyo Bay with eight warships and sails north to establish rival regime at Hakodate, in Hokkaido.

October 23 Era name change, from Keiō to Meiji.

November 6 Defeat of Aizu and northeastern domain alliance leaves imperial army in control of Honshu.

December 22 Tokyo declared open city, allowing foreigners to settle there.

1869 *March 5* Daimyo lords return population and land registers to emperor.

June 27 Defeat of Enomoto's forces at Hakodate ends Boshin Civil War.

1871 *August 29* Abolition of domains and establishment of prefectures.

December 23 Iwakura mission departs Japan for study tour of world.

Questions for Consideration

1. The Tokugawa shogunate was fairly successful in limiting foreign contact with the outside world. Beginning in the late eighteenth century, however, it became increasingly impossible to maintain this policy. What happened in Europe, the United States, and Japan that helped bring about this change?

2. Aizawa Seishisai, the author of *New Theses*, described the foreign threat to Japan in ideological as well as military terms (Document 1). Explain why Aizawa was especially concerned about the threat posed by Christianity. What links can you see between this text written in 1825 and the events that led to the Meiji Restoration in 1868?

3. Even before the arrival of Commodore Perry in 1853, Japanese political leaders and thinkers debated whether or not to broaden diplomatic and commercial relations with foreign countries. What reasons do you think people gave for opening the country? For keeping it closed?

4. Some historians argue that Abe Masahiro's decision to consult the daimyo and others on how to answer the letter from President Millard Fillmore was the beginning of the downfall of the old regime (Document 5). What is the basis of this argument?

5. Discuss Yoshida Shōin's legacy to modern Japan (Document 10). He was executed in 1859 at the age of twenty-nine, but many of his followers went on to play an important role in the Meiji Restoration. After 1868 they continued to be active in military, political, and economic reforms designed to build up Japan's wealth and power. Why were he and his ideas so influential?

6. Yoshida Shōin referred to Napoleon as an ideal leader (Document 10). Yokoi Shōnan and Katsu Kaishū praised the policies of George Washington (Documents 14 and 29). What does this tell you about their different visions of Japan's future? With whom do you agree?

7. In addition to Western heroes, Japanese advocates for reform and revolution such as Aizawa Seishisai, Ōshio Heihachirō, Yoshida Shōin, and Yokoi Shōnan looked to Chinese figures (Documents 1, 2, 10, and 14). What kind of government did Chinese heroes stand for? What are the similarities to

and differences from the Western models alluded to in the previous question?

8. What were the various roles played by women in the drama that led to the Meiji Restoration?

9. Some historians argue that the relaxation of alternative attendance regulations (requiring the daimyo to spend every other year in Edo and his wife and children to live permanently in Edo) in 1862 was the beginning of the downfall of the old regime. What is the basis of this argument?

10. What do satirical songs and reports (Documents 6, 16, 21, and 30) tell us about the political awareness of the common people in Japan? What kinds of ideas did they hold about the shogun, the emperor, the pro-imperial "men of high purpose," and foreigners?

11. In the 1860s, the shogunate was challenged by multiple forces: foreigners demanding trading privileges; "men of high purpose" demanding the expulsion of foreigners and reverence of the emperor; and social unrest among the urban and rural poor in response to bad harvests, inflated commodity prices, and general anxiety over the possibility of war. What would you have done if you were shogun? What do you think of Yoshinobu's decision to return governing authority to the imperial court (Document 28)?

12. The Meiji Restoration marked Japan's birth as a modern nation-state. It involved a transition from a decentralized confederation of some 280 daimyo domains and other estates under the loose control of the shogun to a unified state under the strong control of the emperor. Make comparisons with similar unification movements taking place in Germany and Italy at much the same time (the 1860s and 1870s). Can you identify a common motivating force?

13. In what ways was the Meiji Restoration a revolution comparable to the American Revolution of 1776 or the French Revolution of 1789? In what ways was it different?

14. The outcome of the Meiji Restoration (national unification under the emperor) was not inevitable. Can you imagine other ways Japan might have responded to domestic unrest and foreign challenges in the early and mid-nineteenth century?

15. Discuss the experience of ordinary people in cities and in the countryside in the 1840s, 1850s, and 1860s. What roles did they play in the birth of a new regime? (See especially Documents 3, 22, 23, and 26.)

16. Why did the northeastern domains resist the new imperial government in 1868, even though the former shogun had surrendered (Document 32)?

17. Early in 1868, at the outset of the military campaign against the daimyo supporting the old regime, the pro-imperial forces had the new emperor

sign the Charter Oath, which described the goals of the new government (Document 33). Why do you think the oath was issued at that particular time? The oath refers to getting rid of evil customs of the past. What do you think they were? Contrast the Charter Oath with the injunctions directed at commoners (Document 33). Can you explain why the two documents are so different?

18. If "revere the emperor and expel the barbarians" was the slogan used to attack the Tokugawa government, why did the new imperial government embark on a policy of radical westernization after 1868?

19. Some historians argue that the return of the population and land registers to the national government in 1869, and the abolition of domains and the creation of prefectures in 1871, were the events that made the Meiji Restoration a revolution (Document 34). What is the basis for this argument?

20. The Meiji Restoration was the result of a bloody civil war. Nonetheless, in 1871 Itō Hirobumi gave a speech to the citizens of San Francisco in which he declared: "Within a year a feudal system, firmly established many centuries ago, has been completely abolished, without firing a gun or shedding a drop of blood" (Document 35). Why did Itō paint this "bloodless" picture of the Meiji Restoration, one that has continued to resonate ever since?

Selected Bibliography

GENERAL

Beasley, W. G. *The Meiji Restoration.* Stanford, Calif.: Stanford University Press, 1972.

Jansen, Marius B., and Gilbert Rozman, eds. *Japan in Transition: From Tokugawa to Meiji.* Princeton, N.J.: Princeton University Press, 1986.

Totman, Conrad. *Early Modern Japan.* Berkeley: University of California Press, 1993.

POLITICAL HISTORY

Baxter, James C. *The Meiji Unification through the Lens of Ishikawa Prefecture.* Cambridge, Mass.: Council on East Asian Studies, Harvard University, 1994.

Bolitho, Harold. "The Tempō Crisis." In *The Cambridge History of Japan.* Vol. 5, *The Nineteenth Century,* edited by Marius B. Jansen. Cambridge: Cambridge University Press, 1989.

Craig, Albert M. *Chōshū in the Meiji Restoration.* Cambridge Mass.: Harvard University Press, 1961.

Hall, John W., and Yoshio Sakata. "The Motivation of Political Leadership: The Meiji Restoration." *Journal of Asian Studies* 16, no. 1 (November 1956): 31–50.

Hillsborough, Romulus. *Shinsengumi: The Shogun's Last Samurai Corps.* Rutland, Vt.: Tuttle, 2005.

Jansen, Marius B., ed. *The Cambridge History of Japan.* Vol. 5, *The Nineteenth Century.* Cambridge: Cambridge University Press, 1989.

————. *Sakamoto Ryōma and the Meiji Restoration.* Stanford, Calif.: Stanford University Press, 1961.

Keene, Donald. *Emperor of Japan: Meiji and His World, 1852–1912.* New York: Columbia University Press, 2002.

Ravina, Mark. *The Last Samurai: The Life and Battles of Saigo Takamori.* Hoboken, N.J.: John Wiley & Sons, 2004.

Totman, Conrad. *The Collapse of the Tokugawa Bakufu, 1862–1868.* Honolulu: University of Hawai'i Press, 1980.

Walthall, Anne. "Shipwreck! Akita's Local Initiative, Japan's Foreign Debt, 1869–72." *Journal of Japanese Studies* 39, no. 2 (2013): 271–96.

INTELLECTUAL HISTORY

Harootunian, H. D. *Toward Restoration: The Growth of Political Consciousness in Tokugawa Japan.* Berkeley: University of California Press, 1970.

Huber, Thomas. *The Revolutionary Origins of Modern Japan.* Stanford, Calif.: Stanford University Press, 1981.

Koschmann, J. Victor. *The Mito Ideology: Discourse, Reform, and Insurrection in Late Tokugawa Japan, 1790–1864.* Berkeley: University of California Press, 1987.

Watanabe Hiroshi. *A History of Japanese Political Thought, 1600–1900.* Translated by David Noble. Tokyo: LTCB International Library Trust, International House of Japan, 2012.

Wilson, George M. *Patriots and Redeemers in Japan: Motives in the Meiji Restoration.* Chicago: University of Chicago Press, 1992.

SOCIAL AND ECONOMIC HISTORY

Motoyama Yukihiko. "Patterns of Thought and Action of the Common People during the Bakumatsu and Restoration Epoch." In *Proliferating Talent: Essays on Politics, Thought, and Education in the Meiji Era*, ed. J. S. A. Elisonas and Richard Rubinger, 17–82. Honolulu: University of Hawai'i Press, 1997.

Nenzi, Laura. *The Chaos and Cosmos of Kurosawa Tokiko.* Honolulu: University of Hawai'i Press, 2015.

Silberman, Bernard S. *Ministers of Modernization: Elite Mobility in the Meiji Restoration, 1868–1873.* Tucson: University of Arizona Press, 1964.

Smits, Gregory. *Seismic Japan: The Long History and Continuing Legacy of the Ansei Edo Earthquake.* Honolulu: University of Hawai'i Press, 2013.

Steele, M. William. *Alternative Narratives in Modern Japanese History.* London: RoutledgeCurzon, 2003.

Sugiyama, Shinya. *Japan's Industrialization in the World Economy, 1859–1899: Export Trade and Overseas Competition.* London: Athlone Press, 1988.

Vaporis, Constantine Nomikos. *Tour of Duty: Samurai, Military Service in Edo, and the Culture of Early Modern Japan.* Honolulu: University of Hawai'i Press, 2008.

Walthall, Anne. *The Weak Body of a Useless Woman: Matsuo Taseko and the Meiji Restoration.* Chicago: University of Chicago Press, 1998.

Yamamura, Kozo. "The Founding of Mitsubishi: A Case Study in Japanese Business History." *Business History Review* 41, no. 2 (Summer 1967): 141–60.

———. *A Study of Samurai Income and Entrepreneurship: Quantitative Analyses of Economic and Social Aspects of the Samurai in Tokugawa and Meiji Japan.* Cambridge, Mass.: Harvard University Press, 1974.

PERSONAL ACCOUNTS

Fukuzawa Yukichi. *The Autobiography of Yukichi Fukuzawa*. Translated by Eiichi Kiyooka. New York: Schocken Books, 1972.

Katsu Kokichi. *Musui's Story: The Autobiography of a Tokugawa Samurai*. Translated by Teruko Craig. Tucson: University of Arizona Press, 1988.

McClellan, Edwin. *Woman in the Crested Kimono: The Life of Shibue Io and Her Family Drawn from Mori Ōgai's Shibue Chūsai*. New Haven, Conn.: Yale University Press, 1985.

Shiba Gorō. *Remembering Aizu: The Testament of Shiba Gorō*. Translated by Teruko Craig. Honolulu: University of Hawai'i Press, 1999.

Yamakawa Kikue. *Women of the Mito Domain: Recollections of Samurai Family Life*. Translated by Kate Wildman Nakai. Stanford, Calif.: Stanford University Press, 2001.

FOREIGN AFFAIRS

Assendelft de Coningh, C. T. *A Pioneer in Yokohama: A Dutchman's Adventures in the New Treaty Port*. Translated and edited by Martha Chaiklin. Indianapolis: Hackett, 2012.

Auslin, Michael R. *Negotiating with Imperialism: The Unequal Treaties and the Culture of Japanese Diplomacy*. Cambridge, Mass.: Harvard University Press, 2004.

Barr, Pat. *The Coming of the Barbarians: A Story of Western Settlement in Japan, 1853–1870*. London: Penguin, 1967.

Beasley, W. G. *Japan Encounters the Barbarian: Japanese Travellers in America and Europe*. New Haven, Conn.: Yale University Press, 1995.

Hall, Francis. *Japan through American Eyes: The Journal of Francis Hall, Kanagawa and Yokohama, 1859–1866*. Edited by F. G. Notehelfer. Princeton, N.J.: Princeton University Press, 1992.

Heusken, Henry. *Japan Journal, 1855–1861*. Translated and edited by Jeannette C. van der Corput and Robert A. Wilson. New Brunswick, N.J.: Rutgers University Press, 1964.

Hoare, J. E. *Japan's Treaty Ports and Foreign Settlements: The Uninvited Guests, 1858–1899*. Folkstone, Kent: Japan Library, 1994.

Lensen, George Alexander. *Trading Under Sail Off Japan, 1860 to 1899: The Recollections of Captain John Baxter Will, Sailing-Master and Pilot*. Tokyo: Sophia University Press, 1968.

Perry, Commodore M. C. *Narrative of the Expedition to the China Seas and Japan, 1852–1854*. Mineola, N.Y.: Dover, 2000.

Acknowledgments (*continued from p. iv*)

Document 1: Used by permission of Harvard University Asia Center.

Document 2: Used by permission of the Center for East Asian Studies, University of Chicago.

Document 7: Used by permission of the Institute of Asian Cultural Studies, International Christian University.

Document 10: Used by permission of the Centre for East Asian Cultural Studies, Toyo Bunko.

Document 14: Used by permission of Monumenta Nipponica, Sophia University.

Document 18: Anne Walthall, *The Weak Body of a Useless Woman: Matsuo Taseko and the Meiji Restoration.* © 1998 by The University of Chicago. Used by permission of the University of Chicago Press.

Document 24a: Used by permission of the Institute of Asian Cultural Studies, International Christian University.

Document 26c: Used by permission of the University of Hawai'i Press.

Document 28a: Used by permission of the Centre for East Asian Studies.

Document 30: From *Alternative Narratives in Modern Japanese History*, by M. William Steele. Copyright 2003. Published by Routledge Curzon. Reproduced with permission of Taylor & Francis Books UK.

Document 33a: Used by permission of Monumenta Nipponica, Sophia University.

Document 33b: Used by permission of the Centre for East Asian Cultural Studies, Toyo Bunko.

Document 34a: Used by permission of the University of Tokyo Press.

Index

Abe Masahiro, 12
  debate on opening the country, 52–54
"Abolition of Domains and Creation of Prefectures" (Kido Takayoshi), 145–48
actors (Kabuki), 10, 11, 44–45
agriculture. *See* farmers and agriculture; *specific crops*
Aizawa Seishisai
  commoners, view of, 23
  foreigners, view of, 8
  imperial tombs and, 11
  "New Theses" (*Shinron*) 8, 16, 31–37, 82
Aizu domain, 18, 21–23, 99–102, 129, 137–41
Amaterasu (sun goddess), 2, 32–37
ambassadors, 12–13, 116
animal husbandry, 46
"Appeal on Behalf of Tokugawa Nariaki" (Kurosawa Tokiko), 66–69
"Argument against Civil War" (Katsu Kaishū), 130–33
Arimura Jizaemon, 77
Arisugawa Taruhito, 134–35
Armstrong guns, 21
arson as weapon, 9–10, 18, 99, 102–4, 105*f*
artisans, 5
Ashikaga shoguns, 18, 95–97
Ashikaga Takauji (shogun), 96
Ashikaga Yoshiakira (shogun), 96
Ashikaga Yoshimitsu (shogun), 96
assassinations and executions
  disrespect for emperor and, 17–18, 95–97
  of Emperor Kōmei, suspected, 20
  of foreigners, 93
  during Great Purge, 14–15, 77, 153
  of Ii Naosuke, 15, 77–80, 81*f*, 153
  of Russian tsar, 26
  of Sakamoto Ryōma, 20, 118, 154
  of Yoshida Shōin, 15, 70, 153

Baba Bun'ei, "Chōshū's Attack on the Imperial Palace," 99–103
bathhouses, 47
"black ships," 49–50, 54–56, 55*f*, 110–11
Bonaparte, Napoleon, 7
books, 47
Boshin Civil War (1868–1869), 21, 128–29
  chronology of, 154–55

funding for, 24
  Katsu's argument against, 130–33
  map of, 22*f*
  outcome of, 21–23
  Toba-Fushimi battle, 21, 124, 130, 134, 137, 145, 155
bribery, 38
Britain
  attack on citizens of, 17, 135
  Canada and, 27
  Crimean War (1853–1856), 26
  first contact with Japan, 7, 153
  government of, 86
  navy of, 88
  opium trade and, 58
  Opium War (1839–1842), 7–8, 42
  political reforms in, 26
  risk of war with, 57–59
  trade with, 7–8, 87
  whaling ships of, 7
broadsheets, 54–56, 55*f*, 104, 105*f*, 111–12
Buddhism, 35–36
Bunkyū era (1861–1863) reforms, 16–17
  shogun–daimyo relations, 89–92
  state policy, problems with, 82–88
  woodblock print on, 93–94, 93*f*
burials, 138–39

California, 49, 50, 149
"Call to Arms, A" (Ōshio Heihachirō), 9–10, 37–41
Canada, 27
Catholic missionaries, 6
celebrations, 20, 122–25, 126*f*, 154
ceremonies, religious, 11, 12, 43–44
charity, 108, 112–13
Charter Oath, 23–24
"Charter Oath and Injunctions to Commoners, The," 142–45
children, 138–41
China
  government of, 86
  opium and, 57–58
  Opium War (1839–1842), 7–8, 42
  political reform in, 26
  Russia and, 87
  trade with, 6, 13, 49, 60
  United States, trade with, 51